The
MAKING
of the
SERMON

The
MAKING
of the
SERMON

Robert J. McCracken

HARPER & BROTHERS
New York

Printed in Great Britain
Library of Congress catalog card number: 55-11481

CONTENTS

CONTENTS

PREFACE

❦

O f the making of books about preaching there would seem to be no end. One wonders whether there is any other subject that has had so much written about it. In a field traversed with such thoroughness and in such detail originality is hard to come by; perhaps the most one can hope for is freshness of approach and a working out of the relation of the perennial Gospel to contemporary conditions and needs.

This book owes its existence to an invitation extended by President John A. Mackay to deliver the Stone Lectures at Princeton Seminary. With the invitation there went a suggestion that the lectures should deal with preaching in its practical aspect. It had been my experience in addressing theological students and conferences of ministers that interest was greatest in the actual, week-by-week construction of the sermon. How, men wanted to know, did one budget one's time in preparing for the pulpit? How did one select texts and subjects and gather material for them? What principles should be followed in sermon building?

It is on questions like these that I have concentrated. In the nature of the case much of what is said is personal. For this I make no apology, believing as I do that preaching, to be effective, must be an intensely individual exercise and that "whatever is anonymous won't preach." Those who have a natural gift for preaching, if they should read what follows, may be interested principally in noting how one man goes about the task of making the sermon. Others may find here hints and suggestions which will aid them in cultivating native gifts and deepen their devotion to the preaching office.

It only remains to add that portions of these lectures were delivered at The Southern Baptist Theological Seminary, Louisville, and at the Divinity School of McMaster University, Hamilton, Ontario. I shall long cherish the memory of the gracious hospitality and cordial hearing extended to me by the faculty and students at Princeton, Louisville and McMaster.

ROBERT J. McCRACKEN

The Long-range Preparation of the Sermon

When I had just passed my seventeenth birthday I went to my father and told him I would like to become a minister. There was a long pause after which he made two disconnected remarks which rather daunted me. "Don't think," he said, "that you will be able to please everybody." He then added, "If you get into a pulpit"—the conditional clause was emphatic—"be sure to select a great text."

For what I want to say about the long-range preparation of the sermon I have a relevant as well as a great text. It combines two injunctions of the Apostle Paul: one offered to his son in the faith, Timothy, "Take heed unto thyself, and unto the doctrine" (I Tim. 4:16); the other addressed to the elders of the church in Ephesus, "Take heed . . . to all the flock over which the Holy Spirit has made you overseers" (Acts 20:28).

First and foremost, the preacher is to practice self-discipline. It goes without saying that he will carefully and conscientiously prepare his sermons. He may not feel that he should be in his study, as Alexander Whyte of Free St. George's Church, Edinburgh, did without fail at nine o'clock on Monday morning. All things considered, it might be wiser for him to be in the garden or on the golf course at nine o'clock on Monday morning. I recall a Monday morning when I was on the golf course with three ministers. One of them teed his ball and, addressing it, said, "Elder So-and-so, this has been coming to you for a very long time." And at that, he drove it crisply and cleanly right down the middle of the fairway. We told him that he was exteriorizing his own rottenness. If we were right it was far better that he should be out-of-doors than shut up in his study, nursing his miseries. The point is, however, that while a preacher may not, perhaps should not, be at his desk at nine o'clock on Monday morning, at any rate if he is not an indolent but an industrious workman he will not be found chasing around for a text and a theme late on Friday, or even Saturday, night.

And yet, essential as it is that he should prepare his sermons, it is even more essential that he should prepare himself. Concerning the man who stands in the pulpit Emerson's sentence, trite enough in other connections, is always apposite: "What you are speaks so loud that I cannot hear what you say." There may conceivably be some walks of life in which a man's character has no bearing on the success or failure of his work; the ministry is certainly not one of them. If we do not give heed to the enrichment of character, if with the passage of the years we do not acquire personal weight—I am not thinking of pounds and ounces but of force and strength and distinctiveness of personality—it matters little how eloquent we may be as preachers, our ministry will always convey to the discerning the impression that we lack something vital and indispensable.

A worshiper turned at the conclusion of a sermon and said to his neighbor, "Had this been reported, it would read quite well, yet our friend somehow impresses one as so small that nothing he says carries any weight." What a devastating criticism of a sermon! I used to think I knew the most crushing criticism that could be offered of any sermon. It was made by a student about a sermon preached by a fellow student in the homiletics class. When the time came for appraisal he said, "The sermon was too long by one half, and it does not really matter which half is taken away." That is deadly but not nearly as deadly as, "The preacher impresses one as so small that nothing he says carries any weight."

John Oman, to whom the comment was made, asks us to contrast with it what a reporter wrote about a political speech delivered by the late Viscount Grey. "I think I have reported every word exactly. Indeed few speakers are easier to report, because"—who would take this as a compliment? —"there never is anything unexpected either in form or substance. Yet I know that the report will give no idea of the impression of the speech, for when Grey says it, even the most commonplace utterance seems to carry weight." Intrigued, the reporter went on. "This personal weight is a very mysterious business. When I see Grey in a gathering of small tradesmen and nobodies in this small country town, never putting himself forward, but talking to everyone as his equal, I ask myself, 'Is this the man to whom all the chancelleries in Europe give heed?' But presently I see that everyone recognizes this peculiar personal weight; and that it would be the same anywhere. It is not his position, it is not his reputation, it is not his ability, it is somehow just the man himself."[1] Could the case be better stated? We need able men in the pulpit. We need eloquent men in the pulpit. But most of all we need men of character and principle in the pulpit. Personal quality is the major factor in producing spiritual power.

Somebody once said of Seneca, "His thoughts are excellent, if only he had the right to utter them." Think about that. It is a ghastly business when a man has to go into a pulpit Sunday by Sunday throughout a lifetime and talk about experiences which he himself has never known at first hand. There is no satisfaction in being a weak and faint echo when one should be a strong and clear voice. Emil Brunner says that before he encountered the Theology of Crisis he was like a sandwich-board man parading the streets with an advertisement about a good meal of which he himself stood in sore need. That sort of thing won't hide; sooner or later the people find it out; and when

---

[1] *Concerning the Ministry*, p. 69. This is surely one of the best books about the preaching office ever written.

they cease to respect him, sense spiritual poverty in him, though he may have the eloquence of a Chrysostom, his influence is at an end. There is a searching line in Dante. "Right well hast thou described the composition of this coin, but tell us, hast thou got it in thy pocket?" Or, as Carlyle remarked, "To teach religion the first thing needful, and the last, and indeed the only thing, is to find a man who *has* religion." We must be very sure that we have the thing about which we presume to preach.

If we have it, we shall have something else, a priceless, indispensable qualification in a preacher, a strong, clear sense of vocation and commission. Is there any mortal more pathetic than the preacher who is without that? He is like a ship without a rudder, like a pilot without a compass. "In preaching," says Vinet, "it is more important to have an object than a subject." Consider what it must mean to have to find a subject week in week out, year in year out, when one no longer has any high or commanding object. One's work is then bound to be a dreary round, a mechanical routine—perfunctory prayers, commonplace homilies, polite handshaking, conventional commiseration, endless tea- and coffee-drinking—the tedium, boredom and futility of it all!

Compare with this the exclamation of P. T. Forsyth when he was at the height alike of his powers and his influence: "I would rather be a Congregational minister than a Cabinet minister." Compare with it J. P. Struthers of Greenock, who, when he graduated from Glasgow

University, was offered by Principal Caird a chair of Greek in Australia at £600 a year. He turned the offer down. Astounded, Caird asked, "Will you reject this offer to become a Cameronian minister at £80 a year?" "I can- not help it, Sir," was the reply, "I have made up my mind to be a minister." Struthers had a robust sense of voca- tion and he never lost it.

In Forsyth and Struthers we hear the authentic note. It is in direct line with what we encounter in the Bible. "There was a man *sent* from God, whose name was John" (John 1:6). Isn't that what makes a ministry prophetic, gives it weight and direction and authority? Take the testimony of Amos. "I was an herdman and a gatherer of sycamore fruit: and the Lord *took* me as I followed the flock, and the Lord said unto me, Go, prophesy unto my people Israel" (Amos 7:14-15). Take the testimony of Paul. "I was *apprehended* by Christ Jesus" (Phil. 3:12, R.V.). The verb suggests a hand on the shoulder, an arrest, a person to person encounter. The preacher who can claim such individual apprehension, such immediacy of experience, will never be without a sense of possession by a power greater than his own. Nor will he be at a loss for subject matter about which to preach. He will be immune from the commonest ministerial sin which is pro- fessionalism, saying the appropriate word, doing the cus- tomary thing, because one is expected to say and do it, and not because one is constrained from within to speak and act. If he is in the ministry it will be because he cannot

14

entertain the thought of being in anything else. It will be because he feels, in his own degree, precisely what Paul felt: "The love of Christ constraineth us" (II Cor. 5:14). "Necessity is laid upon me; yea, woe is me, if I preach not the Gospel" (I Cor. 9:16).

"Take heed unto thyself." This comes first and its importance cannot be exaggerated, but with it is linked an exhortation terse and no less emphatic—"and unto the doctrine." The reference to the corpus of Christian truth is markedly objective. It is not this or that man's private property but the possession of the whole Church, and as such it is the preacher's bounden duty and solemn responsibility to get to know it and to propound it. Our office has a strictly representative character. The case has never been more cogently stated than in P. T. Forsyth's inimitable Lyman Beecher lectures, *Positive Preaching and the Modern Mind,* which though delivered before the First World War are as pertinent and relevant as if they had just come off the press. There is no justification, Forsyth urges, for the free lance in the Christian pulpit. Of all places it is the last in which to express purely personal opinions, however original or striking. There is a difference between a pulpit and a platform, a sermon and a lecture, a church and an auditorium. The Christian preacher is not a lineal descendant of the Greek orator. The obligation that rests on him is not, like Socrates, to follow the argument wherever it may lead but, like

Micah, to declare, "Thus saith the Lord." His first business is as the herald of a revelation. He is a man under authority. He has no right to think of the pulpit as his, still less as the place where he can acquire scope for his individuality or a developing ground for his genius. He has a free pulpit in the sense that no man, and no body of men, should cramp his utterance or dictate what he shall say. But his freedom in the pulpit is subject constantly to certain necessary and self-imposed limitations. Every time he enters it he assumes responsibility for the proclamation of a direct, divine commission.

H. G. Wood in his biography of T. R. Glover tells how the Public Orator of Cambridge University when on holiday at Sheringham was as regular in attendance at the Primitive Methodist Chapel as he was at St. Andrew's Church, Cambridge, in term time. "One Easter Sunday a local preacher was occupying the pulpit, a very original old man and much esteemed in the town. In one seat Glover sat with Rendel Harris, W. B. Selbie, Professor Sims Woodhead and others. The old man began by saying he had asked one of them to preach but they wouldn't, so he had to do it himself. 'Now,' he said, 'you mustn't think about the man who is giving you the bread, but about the bread itself.' Rendel Harris was especially pleased and clapped Glover on the knee and said, 'That's the best thing I have heard about preaching—not the man who gives you the bread, but the bread itself.' "[2] It is a sound

[2] H. G. Wood, *Life of T. R. Glover*, p. 151.

16

emphasis. We are not to preach about things as they happen to strike us. Our role is not that of the philosopher, essayist, commentator. There is a deposit of truth; we are to get to know it. There is a rule of faith; we are to expound it. One of the Puritans made a habit of inscribing his name on the flyleaf of every book he purchased, and under his name two sentences: "Thou art a minister of the Word. Mind thy business."

Having this in mind, we shall do well to beware of what has aptly been called "suburban" preaching, the type of preaching that is always out on the circumference of Christian truth. We shall likewise beware of flitting from text to text in the Bible according as casual interest, or idle fancy, or last minute desperation move us. It is our God-given duty to preach regularly and systematically about the basic and perennial themes—the Incarnation and the Atonement, man's exceeding sinfulness and God's exceeding grace, the life of faith and the life everlasting. These are weighty and profound themes. The first impulse of a minister, and not only of a young minister, is to touch on them lightly or to leave them alone, and this is the reason for the religious illiteracy so prevalent today. In *The Autobiography* Mark Rutherford describes an elderly minister of his acquaintance who had given up preaching on such themes altogether as too complex and bewildering both for himself and his hearers. As a younger man theology and philosophy had engrossed him, but all that was over and done with. He had taken up astronomy as a pastime and on most Sundays exhorted his congregation either to be good or to do good. There is more of this sort of thing in churches than is generally realized. Topical preaching of a moralistic character, divorced from evangelical insights and without a solid biblical or doctrinal basis, is not uncommon. " 'Mony an hungry, starving creature,' said the blind Covenanter woman to Morton in Scott's *Old Mortality,* 'when he sits down on a Sunday forenoon to get something that might warm him to his great work, has a dry clatter o' morality driven about his lugs.' "[3] To deal with the pivotal themes of the Evangel, to "take heed unto the doctrine," we must keep on subjecting ourselves to a vigorous self-discipline. But if we do it we shall, in the words of Scripture, save ourselves as well as our hearers.

One criticism directed not unfairly against a great deal of contemporary preaching is that though relevant and timely in its way, and sometimes well-expressed and well-delivered, little actually comes of it. In view of the thousands upon thousands of sermons preached in the United States on any Sunday, it is disconcerting to think how, when Monday comes, life goes on its way pretty much as before. If we take the situation described in the Book of Acts when the Apostles preached the difference could not be more pronounced. The thing that is lacking is the dynamism of the Gospel. The trouble with much preaching is that it fails either to kindle the mind or to energize the will. It seldom disturbs the conscience or stirs the heart.

[3] Quoted by John Baillie in *Invitation to Pilgrimage,* pp. 50-51.

As we compose our Sunday discourses we need to keep reminding ourselves that moralistic exhortation is not enough, any more than intellectual authoritativeness is enough. The revival of biblical theology, so widespread in our time, if it avoids the scholastic tendency, keeps close to the needs of men and society and to the heart of the Gospel, should result in dynamic preaching.

"Take heed unto thyself, and unto the doctrine, *and to all the flock over which the Holy Spirit has made you overseers.*" Cultivate the shepherd heart. Be a conscientious visitor and pastor. Never lose the human touch. If you can lay hands on it read and reread J. H. Jowett's little book, *A Passion for Souls.* There is a close connection between pastoral and pulpit work. Fidelity in the one may well lead to outstanding power and usefulness in the other. "Now and then we hear it suggested," writes W. R. Bowie, "that the work of the ministry should be so arranged that some men should have nothing to do but preach. 'Let these individuals who are gifted in utterance be set free from other duties,' someone says, 'so that they may spend all their time developing the finest sermons which can be produced.' That sounds like a plausible idea, but it is one which would very soon perish if put to the test. Real sermons do not grow out of academic air any more than roses will bloom cut off from their roots. A man may give his people learned doctrines and even bright theological and ethical curiosities for their intellects to play with if his preaching comes out of his own unrelated life; but if he is to feed their souls, he must preach out of an awareness of the everyday living which he has seen and shared with them."[4]

The case of Dick Sheppard is particularly relevant in this connection. He never lost the human touch. His friends used to be indignant because, plagued as he was by asthma, offering the asthmatics' prayer "Give us this day our daily breath," carrying a cross of a personal kind that was even heavier than asthma, he loaded himself with the burdens of others. He was swift to hear about and to succor some who had never experienced a tithe of the suffering of the man who hurried to their rescue. He would sit up all night with a sick parishioner. Between bouts of illness he would travel all over the country addressing hundreds of meetings, a smile on his face that somehow hid the pallor that was there. When he was Dean of Canterbury he would be up to meet the Cathedral workers on their way to work at six-thirty in the morning. He spent himself on people. He literally gave himself away. What he gained in stature was unmistakable; what others gained from him was immeasurable. Expendable people are always people of tremendous influence. There was the East London dock worker who said, "Good Gawd, Mother, what shall we do without 'im?" And when he died the thing that people discovered they were saying was not, I was so fond of him, but rather, He was so fond of me. There is no doubt at all that this fellow-feeling, this self-identification with human

[4] *Preaching*, p. 29.

need, was the strength of his preaching and the secret of his hold on people.[5]

The pastoral instinct, like the preaching instinct, is largely a matter of native endowment. Yet it can be developed and cultivated in the most remarkable way. Men who by disposition and temperament are diffident and reserved have schooled themselves to be outgoing and acquired an interest in people and in their problems, a genuine concern for them and for their happiness and well-being, that have freed them from awkwardness and self-consciousness. In nearly every instance this is productive of results in the matter of church attendance. There is an old saying that a home-going minister makes a church-going congregation. About another type of man people in Scotland are accustomed to say with an air of contemptuous finality: "He suffers from foot and mouth disease; he can't preach and he won't visit." A minister once told an inquiring pulpit deputation that they could not have both brains and boots. Presumably he meant that brains are needed for the pulpit while pastoral work requires only pedestrian qualities. If so, he thereby demonstrated that he had no firsthand acquaintance with the cure of souls, or he would have known its infinite complexity and its call for highly skilled workmen.

Most of us would agree that a minister who can't think, and think clearly, is soon unwanted, but a minister who assumes that he ought to succeed because he can think, and who neglects and even ignores the pastoral and human

[5] See R. Ellis Roberts, *H. R. L. Sheppard, Life and Letters.*

demands made on him, is liable also soon to be unwanted. During your seminary course you have no doubt become familiar with many a definition of religion. It would be a thousand pities if you were to overlook the very practical definition supplied by the Epistle of James: "Pure religion before God and the Father is this, to visit the fatherless and widows in their affliction, and to keep himself unspotted from the world" (James 1:27). Much as you may love to preach, do not disregard your pastoral responsibilities. Ask God to give you a passion for the souls of your people. Are you familiar with the lines F. W. H. Myers puts on the lips of Paul?

Only like souls I see the folk thereunder,
Bound who should conquer, slaves who should be kings,
Hearing their one hope with an empty wonder,
Sadly contented with a show of things.

Then with a rush the intolerable craving
Shivers throughout me like a trumpet call,
O, to save these, to perish for their saving,
Die for their life, be offered for them all.[6]

I hope you find it hard to be a preacher. I trust you will always be conscious of the burden of the ministerial office. The man who does his work effortlessly in the pulpit, and is unaware there of any tension, is not to be envied. There is little likelihood that he will move his hearers mightily. How can he when he himself is not mightily

[6] F. W. H. Myers, *Saint Paul*, p. 40.

moved? Alexander Whyte once surprised his Edinburgh congregation by telling them: "I would flee the pulpit if I only could. Often when the church officer is bringing in the Bible I think of escaping by the back door. You will not believe me, but it's true. And when you are settling your-selves down in your luxurious seats I am holding on by the banister behind me and am pleading with God that He would not cast me away from His presence but would up-hold me with His free spirit. And while the organist wel-comes you in with sweet music I am staggering in with the prayer, 'O sprinkle the pulpit, and the preacher, and the sermon, with the peace speaking and the power giving blood.'" If you think that exaggerated language you neither begin to understand Alexander Whyte nor the sources of his tremendous spiritual influence. In every generation those who know what the Old Testament prophets called "the burden of the Lord" are mightly sustained by the Lord.

Some years ago three ministers foregathered on holiday, and the talk began to run on college days and finally con-centrated on a much loved teacher. One of them, speaking by common consent for all three, said, "Whenever I feel my light burning low and my ideals growing faint, no voice rallies me like the voice of James Denney." It is a tribute which brings me back to the point from which I started. Personal quality is the secret of spiritual power. What you are will speak louder than anything you may say. "The best of God's servants," Mahomet once remarked, "are those who when seen remind of God."

The Varied Character of the Sermon (1)

The story is told about a minister walking home from church on Sunday night, his hands clasped behind his back, his eyes riveted on the ground as if at any moment he might come upon a sixpence, muttering to himself as he went along, "Two more, two more." One Sunday over he was already apprehensive about the approach of another. He must surely have been a man close to the edge of mental and spiritual bankruptcy, in Thoreau's phrase living a life of quiet desperation. Many a time I have wondered as I have thought about such a hand-to-mouth existence what his approach to sermon-making was. Did his sermons all the year round conform more or less to one stereotyped pattern, or were they varied in their character and structure as well as in their content?

I raise the question having two things in mind. One is the problem of coverage. Every preacher should aim to be able to say what Paul told the elders at Ephesus, "I have not shunned to declare unto you all the counsel of God" (Acts 20:27). He should set himself to traverse the entire ground of Christian truth, and to do it systematically, periodically and as comprehensively as he knows how. The other is that of the man who looks forward to an extended ministry in one charge, a ministry, say, of ten or more years, the type of ministry which is most likely to make a real and lasting impact on individuals and the community at large. How is he to avoid repetition, not merely of sermons but of ideas, emphases, terminology? What can he do to keep his thought fresh and his speech unhackneyed? A preacher of originality and distinction, whose name would register with you at once if I mentioned it, told me that as he faced retirement and looked back over the preaching of forty years, the impression grew on him that he had been reiterating, re-emphasizing and reminting about seven leading ideas! The estimate, I suggested, was decidedly on the conservative side, but it helps to explain the lament, "Two more, two more."

These are considerations particularly pertinent for those of us who are ministers of churches which place us under no official obligation to observe the seasons of the Church Year. Even though we are not required to do it, it is a wholesome discipline in our preaching to follow the main· outline of the Church Year—Advent, Christmas, Lent, Good Friday, Easter, Whitsunday, Trinity. It protects us from aimless, haphazard, random utterance, from putting a congregation completely at the mercy of our own homiletical inclinations and predilections, from turning for subject matter to such ephemeral sources as magazines, digests and newspapers. It gives direction as well as inclusiveness to our preaching.

We can secure the comprehensive coverage, especially necessary in the case of an extended ministry, if we make a practice of following a clearly devised pattern in sermon construction. One pattern lies ready to hand and commends itself because of the range and scope it offers. The sermon can be, in turn, expository, ethical, devotional, theological, apologetical, social, psychological, evangelical. No sermon, of course, need rigidly or wholly be any one of these. It may at one and the same time be expository in its basis, ethical in its temper, evangelical in its appeal. Many sermons contain elements of all the types I have enumerated. For the most part, however, if we are aiming at comprehensiveness, they should follow one pattern in the main, should be distinctly expository, or social, or apologetical in character.

There are ministers so accustomed to one type of preaching that they are not only disinclined to attempt any other but are apt to be critical of any other. With one it is religion in its devotional aspect, with another it is the social application of the Gospel, with yet another it is the ethical demands of Christianity. Two points may be urged in this connection.

No preacher should disparage a fellow preacher because he puts the major emphasis on a different aspect of Christian truth. There are diversities of ministry as well as of gifts. At one time on Fifth Avenue, New York, two men were engaged in powerful preaching ministries. They were Harry Emerson Fosdick and John Henry Jowett. Both men preached every Sunday to crowded congregations. Both men lifted the level of life for great numbers of people. Yet their preaching was in marked contrast—Fosdick, a master in Christian apologetics, seeking to interpret the Christian faith in twentieth-century terms, perpetually involved in theological controversy; Jowett, a master in preaching of the devotional sort, concentrating almost exclusively on personal religion and on the deepening of the spiritual life, his orthodoxy taken by everybody for granted. For a study in contrasts read the printed sermons of the two men.

A case no less striking was that of Alexander Maclaren of Manchester and R. W. Dale of Birmingham. Maclaren was a prince among biblical expositors. To this day his sermons are models of expository preaching at its best. He stays with his text, gets the substance out of it, makes an application of it that is as practical and relevant as it is personal. But one thing about the exposition compels attention at once. It is the comparative absence of contemporary reference, of anything that can be described as topical. You will go to Maclaren in vain if you want to know what was happening in Manchester or Britain or the world while he exercised his ministry. In this sense his sermons are not dated, which may be one reason why he has been so much plagiarized. Dale, by comparison, was a topical preacher.

His sermons unfailingly have a biblical basis but contemporary references are to be found on page after page.
Politics, municipal and national, was in the foreground
of his thinking, and the relation and relevance of the
Christian faith to political life and activity was a subject
he returned to again and again. With Maclaren the
dominant interest was biblical; with Dale it was more
varied, was biblical, ethical, social, and all in one. There
are diversities of ministry as well as of gifts. No preacher
should minimize the contribution made by a fellow
preacher because of the difference between them in subject
matter or characteristic emphasis.

But equally, no preacher should strain and tire a congregation by adhering in season and out of season to one
pattern of preaching and one alone. Maclaren, it is true,
concentrated throughout a lifetime on biblical exposition,
but he was a genius the like of which appears only at long
intervals. We should not too readily conclude that we have
the kind of special endowment and all-round brilliance
Maclaren had. For the life of me I cannot comprehend
how some men confine themselves solely to the psychological type of sermon, or how others Sunday after Sunday
keep hammering away at some aspect or other of the social
question. T. R. Glover's biographer quotes him as saying:
"It may be a sign of old age to look back to the Gospel
of my youth and boyhood, but at sixty-six I feel the need
of Some One who will care for me and be with me and be

interested in my thoughts and temptations and will not exclusively harangue me on public issues."[1]

What is needed is that we should deliberately set ourselves to vary the approach in our preaching. If I may venture a personal reference, I find myself at intervals altering the stress from Sunday to Sunday. Some time ago I preached a sermon of an apologetical character, taking for the title, "How Difficult Not to Believe in God!" Preachers deal repeatedly with the problem, How Believe in God in a World like This? In the sermon in question the approach was of a quite different nature. It dealt with the factors—the beauty of the world, the innate goodness of people, the significance of Christ—which make theism not only credible but compelling. This was followed by a sermon in which the emphasis was ethical and social entitled, "Getting Rid of Our Prejudices." Here one had an opportunity of dealing faithfully with religious and racial prejudice, the starting point being Peter's exclamation, "Not so, Lord; for I have never eaten anything that is common or unclean" (Acts 10:14). This in turn was succeeded by a sermon of a biblical and devotional character which I called, "Keeping in Touch with Our Unseen Environment," with for the text the words of Elisha at Dothan, "Lord, I pray Thee, open his eyes that he may see" (II Kings 6:17). If our preaching is to arouse and sustain interest we must keep varying its character along

[1] Op. cit., p. 151.

the line of the eightfold pattern mentioned earlier. About this I now propose to say something in detail.

EXPOSITORY PREACHING

This should have pride of place. For Protestants the Bible is the supreme rule of faith and practice. Yet ignorance of it is so widespread that more than ever it is our duty to expound it. There was a lady who found herself seated at dinner next to a bishop. Thinking to keep the conversation running along channels that would be congenial to a bishop, she asked him what his favorite text in the Bible was. To her dismay he turned the question back on her and insisted that he would prefer instead to learn what her favorite text was. It is to be doubted whether she had one. In any event, there was a rather long pause, but then, rallying and brightening, she replied that the text in the Bible that had always specially appealed to her was, "They also serve who only stand and wait." "And what, my Lord," she repeated, "is your favorite text?" Whereupon, without even the suggestion of a smile, the bishop answered, "God tempers the wind to the shorn lamb." One grows less and less sure in telling it that the story will be appreciated as it ought to be. Even seminary students have been known to fail to grasp the point that neither quotation is from the Bible, the first being from John Milton and the second from Laurence Sterne. Because people by and large are so little acquainted with the Bible it is incumbent upon the preacher to do all he can to make them more familiar with "the lively oracles of God."

When biblical exposition is frequent and systematic it delivers a man from indulging his own predilections. There is a type of topical preaching which results in a congregation being introduced to practically all the strongly held views and nostrums of its minister. All his personal and indeed idiosyncratic thinking about contemporary issues— political and economic as well as religious—is passed on to his people. He has no standard frame of reference. The fact is he has forgotten that there is a supreme rule for faith and practice. He gets his sermons from current events and has little skill in bringing biblical insights to bear on them because his use of the Bible is incidental and marginal. It is not so much a sourcebook as a compendium of handy quotations, a religious scrapbook. Sometimes he writes the sermon and when it is finished consults a concordance with a view to finding an appropriate text. At other times the sermon not only has no text but has nothing to distinguish it from an essay or a newspaper editorial. The danger then is that a minister, almost in complete independence of the Bible, may constitute himself an amateur economist, a social reformer, a practitioner in the art of mental healing, an adviser in all the complicated intricacies of love, courtship and marriage. To engage in serious and systematic biblical exposition frees preaching from the worst kind of subjectivism and gives it breadth and comprehensiveness.

It provides the preacher, moreover, with limitless source material. With the Old and the New Testaments to draw upon, who, if he has any homiletical instinct at all, need go home on Sunday night lamenting, "Two more, two more"? What Dryden said about Chaucer applies in infinitely greater degree to the Bible: "Here is God's plenty." Many a newly ordained minister is startled before long to discover that he has exhausted himself in topical preaching. James Black in *The Mystery of Preaching*, one of the outstanding books on the subject, describes the plight that befell him when he had been no more than a few months in his first charge. He had been preaching on successive Sundays about such subjects as God and man and sin and salvation and prayer and character and citizenship. Soon he felt that he had covered the ground, that there was little more to say, and he wondered in a despairing way how he could ever sustain a ministry in one parish over even a short term of years. He found the answer, as his book admirably illustrates, in expository preaching. The Bible proved a veritable mine, a rich treasury, to which through the long years in a pulpit made famous by another able expositor he could keep turning, confident that the supply would never be exhausted.[2]

By expository preaching I have in mind, first and chiefly, the exposition of a single text. Consider, for instance, one of the greatest of the New Testament doxologies: "Unto Him that loveth us, and loosed us from our sins by His blood, and hath made us kings and priests unto God and His Father; to Him be the glory and the dominion for ever and ever" (Rev. 1:5, 6). Here the divisions are ready to

[2] P. 139.

hand. No time has to be spent in devising them or in arranging them in proper sequence. They are three in number and cumulative as they stand. He loves us. He loosed us from our sins. He has made us kings and priests. In working out in contemporary terminology the implications of those tremendous affirmations we are close to the heart of the Gospel and should be able to provide our hearers with an account, clear and comprehensive, of what Christ does for the soul that trusts Him. Or, consider a definitive statement like that of John 7:17: "If any man will do His will, he shall know of the doctrine, whether it be of God or whether I speak of myself." This, if ever there was one, is a sweeping generalization. It is all-inclusive and admits of no exceptions. It suggests a sermon with one leading thought which it is the preacher's business to unfold, elaborate, illustrate and apply. Obedience is the organ of spiritual knowledge. Doing and knowing are blood relations. People say, First I must know, then I will do. The reverse is the case. Christianity begins as an experiment and ends as an experience. "I wish I had your creed, then I would live your life," a seeker after truth remarked to Pascal. And swift as a rapier thrust came the reply, "Live my life and you will soon have my creed."

The exposition may be not of a single but of a multiple text. Two Old Testament sentences, in striking contrast, can be used with telling effect as themes for a sermon: "And he [Samson] wist not that the Lord had departed from him" (Judg. 16:20), and, "Moses wist not that the

33

skin of his face shone" (Exod. 34:29). Says the one, spiritual deterioration can be unconscious. A man, morally, can go downhill, with others aware of the fact, but he himself oblivious to the danger he is in until a crisis shocks him into self-knowledge. Says the other, the height of spiritual loveliness is to be lovely and not to know it. The greatest saints are always positive that they are the chief of sinners. When a man suspects that he is good he begins to be bad. In a sermon of this kind the findings of psychology can be drawn upon in applying the insights of Scripture . . . Another combination of texts which affords material for a helpful discourse is: "Every man shall bear his own burden" (Gal. 6:5), "Bear ye one another's burdens" (Gal. 6:2), "Cast thy burden upon the Lord" (Ps. 55:22). The task facing the preacher in such a case is straightforward. The groundwork has been done for him. What the Bible has to say about a problem affecting all his hearers is concise and explicit. All that remains for him to do is to take the truth and expound it in terms that are illuminating and self-evidencing.

A much more difficult task is that of expounding a passage in the Bible, Paul's prison prayer, for example, in Ephesians 3:13 f., or one of the Psalms, say the 23rd or the 46th. This can best be done in situations where an initial interest can be assumed, if one is addressing people who want to be informed about the meaning and message of the Bible. Even then, to do it well, so that what is said is significant, relevant and applicable is a formidable undertaking. Some do it in such commonplace and un-inspired fashion that one is tempted to suggest that they had better leave it alone. Yet it can be done well and should be attempted. This is where masters of biblical exposition— George Adam Smith, Alexander Maclaren, J. H. Jowett, George Buttrick—may be studied with profit.

Because ignorance of its contents is so widespread a preacher renders a real service who devotes himself in a single sermon to the exposition of a book of the Bible. Some lend themselves more readily to such treatment than others. It would be next to impossible to do justice in one utterance to a book of the size and scope of Genesis, or to any one of the Gospels. But there are smaller books whose message can be brought within the compass of a single sermon. Thus one might base a sermon on the Book of Ruth with some such title as "Triumphing over Racial Prejudice," and follow it with a companion sermon based on the Book of Jonah and entitled, "Triumphing over Religious Prejudice." Or one might preach a sermon on the Book of Nehemiah—what a stirring piece of writing it is!—and call it, "An Experiment in Social Reconstruction." As for the New Testament, any man with imagination and the human touch can preach a moving and timely sermon on the Epistle to Philemon, one of the most charming letters ever written, giving it a title like, "A First-century Solution of an Age-old Social Problem." Exposition of this sort opens up the Bible as a living document to many for whom it would otherwise be only

35

ancient literature, treated with conventional deference but unread.

At regular intervals a place should be made for sustained and systematic exposition involving a series of sermons. Why not preach one's way, clause by clause, through the Beatitudes, the Lord's Prayer, the Ten Commandments, and, in Lent, the Seven Last Words? It might be well instead of dealing with each clause on successive Sundays to take them on a stated Sunday in successive months. This would apply even more to a sermon course on the Parables, or to a series of biographical studies of the Twelve Apostles, or to a sequence of addresses on The Sermon on the Mount. There is an abundance of source material for all of these. To name only one significant contribution in each field there is Percy Ainsworth for the Beatitudes, Studdert-Kennedy for the Lord's Prayer, Sloane Coffin for the Ten Commandments, J. D. Jones for the Twelve Apostles, George Buttrick for the Parables, Bishop Gore for the Sermon on the Mount. In working on themes like these we have the satisfaction not only of knowing where we are going but of dealing with issues fundamental to the Christian religion.

It cannot be overemphasized that the primary consideration in biblical exposition is to maintain interest and keep close to life. The weakness of much expository preaching is twofold; it inclines to be tedious and colorless, and it is often detached and remote from the activities and concerns of everyday existence. Nobody will deny

the industry and conviction back of it, but it lacks relevance
and contemporaneity.

> A parish-priest of austerity,
> Climbed up in a high Church-steeple
> To be nearer God, that he might hand
> His Word down to the people.
>
> And in sermon-script he daily wrote
> What he *thought* was sent from heaven,
> And dropped it down on the people's heads
> Two times one day in seven!
>
> In his age, God said "Come down and die,"
> And he cried out from his steeple,
> "Where art Thou, Lord?" and the Lord replied,
> "Down here among My people"![3]

The pathos amounting to tragedy in those lines lies in
the fact that the parish priest was not an idler. He was
conscientious and industrious, but for all that an intellectual alien. He was out of touch with the currents of life
and thought round about him. He had apparently never
learned to apply biblical insights to contemporary situations.
The remedy for all such detachment is indicated in the
experience of Ezekiel. He was in Babylon, an exile
addressing exiles. He was sent there by the express
command of God. He went, not without reluctance, to

[3] Quoted by Adam W. Burnet in *Pleading with Men*, pp.
112-13.

the captives by the river Chebar and took his place by their side. "I sat where they sat," he says. What Ezekiel found was that before he could be of service to people he had to put himself in their place. He had to live as they were living, to feel as they were feeling, to become sensitive to every current of the life round about him. Fellow-feeling, self-identification—those are the essentials of effective expository preaching.

The Varied Character of the Sermon (2)

❦

Expository preaching should have pride of place, and for this reason, I have devoted the greater part of an entire lecture to it. But if it is to be varied and comprehensive, preaching should also follow other patterns. To the consideration of these we turn now.

ETHICAL PREACHING

About religion and morality it cannot too often be said, "What God hath joined together, let not man put asunder" (Matt. 19:6). It is impossible to miss the stress on the moral demand in the Prophets, the Gospels and the Epistles. One hears many sermons criticized nowadays on the ground that they are moralistic. The criticism is justified if a moral demand is made and nothing is said about the divine grace which is available in the Gospel of Christ, empowering men to translate the ideal into the actual. Morality divorced from religion creates the predicament Paul faced, and Augustine after him, and Luther after him: "The good that I would, I do not: but the evil which I would not, that I do" (Rom. 7:19). Christianity is first and foremost a Gospel, "the power of God unto salvation," but without "works" it is dead. If it does not produce grace and strength and integrity of character it is worthless.

Dick Sheppard used to reiterate that if Jesus Christ cannot make character He can make nothing else. It was a deliberately provocative way of stating the case, but on what grounds can it be challenged? Nothing so discredits religion as a profession and a practice at variance, whether at the individual, the congregational, or the national level. Preaching which was unethical in substance, and which therefore failed to beget a strong moral sense, provoked from John Wesley this outburst: "I find more profit in sermons on either good tempers, or good works, than in what are vulgarly called Gospel sermons. That term has now become a mere cant word: I wish none of our society would use it. It has no determinate meaning. Let but a pert, self-sufficient animal, that has neither sense nor grace, bawl out something about Christ, or His blood, or justification by faith, and his hearers cry out: 'What a fine Gospel sermon!' "[1]

The point is well taken. How does one apply it? Present your congregation some Sunday morning with a plea for kindness. It is the vitamin of the soul for which multitudes everywhere hunger. Often it is in astonishingly short

[1] *Works* (edit. 1872), Vol. XIII, p. 36; quoted in W. E. Sangster, *The Craft of Sermon Construction*, p. 31.

supply. In great cities in particular where contacts tend to be impersonal and human need can go unrelieved and even unnoticed it is a subject calling for frequent emphasis. Take for your text, "Be ye kind one to another" (Eph. 4:32), and for your title, "Majoring in a Minor Virtue." (By the time the sermon is preached you may feel that the virtue is not minor but major.) I did it once and the next day saw that *The New York Times* had given three quarters of a column to what I had to say. Who would have thought that a simple plea for kindness rated such space in the first section of a great metropolitan newspaper?

Or, some Sunday, getting down to ethical bedrock, select for your subject "Reality in Religion," and for a text draw on Micah's extraordinarily succinct summarization: "What doth the Lord require of you but to do justly, and to love mercy, and to walk humbly with thy God" (Mic. 6:8). Even if by some mischance in the handling of it you should bungle a magnificent opportunity, think what the congregation will have to carry away with it. The divisions, three in number, are ready to hand. And what divisions! Justice, tempered with mercy, inspired by daily communion with God. Some, you will point out, are upright as a marble column and as cold and as hard. You may cite the case of Lachlan Campbell in Ian Maclaren's *Beside the Bonnie Brier Bush*. In any event, you will bring out the moral contradiction, show how it can be resolved, and how in resolving it we get to the core of real religion.

If you have in mind ethical preaching involving a

41

personal encounter, go some Sunday to the Psalter and in all you say concentrate on the words, "Who can understand his errors? cleanse thou me from secret faults" (Ps. 19:12). Such a sermon, for which you might borrow Douglas Steere's title, *On Beginning from Within*, is likely to be psychological as well as ethical in its tone and temper. You will have to bring out that the Psalmist is thinking, not of faults well-known to himself and skillfully concealed from others, but of faults of which he himself is altogether unconscious. Because it deals with self-anatomy, this should be preaching of the probing, surgical sort. It should lead your hearers to ask the kind of question put by the small boy to his mother after he had been listening to Charles Haddon Spurgeon for no more than a matter of minutes, "Mother, is Mr. Spurgeon speaking to me?"

On occasion, despite the old saying that a sermon without a text is a pretext, you may go into the pulpit with a topic like, "Wanted! A New Moral Sense!" While no word of Scripture is announced at the outset it will be a gross dereliction of duty if biblical insights, clearly enunciated and cogently applied, are not what distinguishes everything you say from newspaper and magazine articles on the same, much-discussed subject. The individual will not be forgotten but attention will be focused on our generation's blind spot, the disparity between material and spiritual progress, the lag between scientific development and moral knowledge. Science, it will be emphasized, is daily putting into our hands greater and still greater powers, but unless there is an advance in moral character to correspond with the technical advance the results are bound to be calamitous. In all this the strongest point to urge will be that made some time ago by the physicist in a state university who said: "I have come to three conclusions. The first is that salvation is not to be found in science. Secondly, we must have a moral revival. Thirdly, we can have no moral revival without a living religion."

Devotional Preaching

This falls under two main heads. *There are sermons whose design is the deepening of the spiritual life.* For preaching of this nature some men have a special aptitude. My background being Scottish I think at once of Alexander Smellie, A. J. Gossip, James S. Stewart. Even to read their sermons in cold print is to be stirred at the deepest levels to renewed endeavor and aspiration. Joseph Fort Newton seems to me to have had the same striking gift. I never heard him preach but, speaking for myself, I know of few preachers who can so quickly evoke and sustain a spiritual mood. Harry Emerson Fosdick in this aspect of his pulpit work, as indeed in every other, excels. *The Meaning of Prayer* is a gem of devotional literature and likely in years to come to rank with the classics in the field. Masters like these may be used as models. By observing their choice of subjects, treatment of texts, use of illustrations, distribution of emphasis, we can learn how best to prepare the type of address in which we inspire our hearers to go further by enabling them to go deeper.

Distinct from this is the sermon whose *design is comfort and inspiration*. In the hands of a man who has sympathy and insight, think of what can be made of passages in the Bible superlatively rich in promise and assurance. "The name of the Lord is a strong tower: the righteous runneth into it, and is safe" (Prov. 18:10). "And Jonathan arose, and went to David in the wood, and strengthened his hand in God" (I Sam. 23:16). "My grace is sufficient for thee: for My strength is made perfect in weakness" (II Cor. 12:9). I cite these, not haphazardly and at random, nor because they are familiar passages and have been the subject of countless inspirational sermons, but because when an undergraduate at Glasgow University over thirty years ago I heard George H. Morrison of the Wellington Church expound them, and the memory of what he made of them and of the stimulus they imparted lingers to this day. John Watson is said to have remarked to an intimate friend toward the end of his life that if he had his ministry to exercise over again he would preach more comforting sermons. Asked for the reason the reply he gave was that most people are fighting a hard battle. They are indeed. They are battling with fear, insecurity, doubt, temptation. They are trying to find sense and meaning in a world so rent with rivalries and antagonisms that the foundations of ordered life are sagging. Nevertheless, over against the dictum of John Watson, it is well, if preaching is to keep balance and proportion, to set the observation of Cardinal Newman, "Christianity is a cordial, but no one drinks cordials from morning until night." Watson sensed the need of preaching more comforting sermons, but his ministry would have lost perspective if he had preached only comforting sermons.

Theological Preaching

Even allowing for the revived interest in theology and the influence of neo-orthodoxy, here is where American preaching, by and large, is weakest. The impression is prevalent among us that a doctrinal sermon in the nature of the case can hardly be other than ponderous, if not dull, and that to our practical-minded people it is bound to seem abstruse and academic.

In point of fact theological preaching need have none of these characteristics. Its business is to answer the most basic questions men are capable of asking. In times like these men want to know whether the universe is friendly, and whether life has purpose and meaning; and theology answers with a doctrine of God. They want to know whether man is able to apprehend the meaning of life, and to ally himself with God in fellowship and service; and the answer given by theology is a doctrine of Man. They want to know how the essential meaning of life is disclosed to man; and in reply theology offers a doctrine of Revelation. They want to know how life can be redeemed from frustration and futility and lifted to its highest levels;

D   45

and theology comes forward with a doctrine of Salvation. There is nothing necessarily pedantic or scholastic in all this. These are live issues and they are the very stuff out of which theology is made. Not only so, they are the stuff out of which the best preaching is made. It is sheer tragedy when preaching on such perennial themes is supplanted by topical chitchat, or elaborate liturgies, or by programs of religious education prolific in techniques but woefully deficient in genuine religious content. A deacon commented to a visiting minister about his own recently appointed pastor: "Our young man has settled a lot of problems we never heard of, and answered a lot of questions nobody was asking." To which the visiting minister replied, "Your pastor is evidently a thoughtful lad and will come to the right place with experience." But in his private mind what he thought was: "If that young fellow had been grappling with the basic doctrines of the New Testament he would have been nearer the sources of power and infinitely more helpful to his people."

Theological preaching is deservedly unpopular if all it does is settle a lot of problems people never heard of, and answer a lot of questions nobody ever asks. Actually, in the pews facing us Sunday after Sunday are men and women who want to know the why and wherefore of the Christian faith. That they are theologically illiterate is our fault above and beyond that of anybody else. They are asking for more than running commentaries on current affairs, for more than repeated exhortations, couched in vague and general terms, to be better Christians. Were it expressed vividly and in language they could follow and comprehend they would be interested to learn what to believe and why. A series of sermons on the teaching of Jesus about God, man, sin, forgiveness would keep preaching Christocentric and edify as well as instruct our congregations. The majority of people believe in "some sort of a Something." If it is the case that the question is not, Is there a God? but What is He like? a succession of sermons on the attributes of God—His omnipresence, with for the biblical source Psalm 137; His omnipotence, with for the text the concluding clause of the Lord's Prayer, "Thine is the Kingdom and the Power and the Glory forever and ever"; His holiness, the point of departure the sixth chapter of Isaiah—would do much to clarify and objectify thought. To help church members become theologically literate it would be a rewarding exercise, as much for the preacher as for those he addresses, to study, clause by clause, the Apostles' Creed. If for a young minister, or at the beginning of a pastorate, this should be reckoned too exacting, individual sermons of a doctrinal character could be made a fixed feature of the Church Year, with titles like the following: How Do You Think of God?, What Is Meant by the Divinity of Christ?, What Are We to Make of Man?, Why Did Jesus Die?

Theological preaching is an absolute necessity. As rational beings we are under obligation to reflect on our experience and seek to understand it. By itself, the practical side of religion cannot finally satisfy us; we must have an interpretation of it. Without it there can be no intellectual self-respect. What, after all, is theology but ordered thinking, some would say scientific thinking, about God and man and the world and the relations between them? Men everywhere have an unquenchable desire to understand the scheme of things in which they find themselves. This is the task to which we apply ourselves when the theological emphasis in the sermon is pronounced.

Apologetical Preaching

The need for this arises because of the fact, familiar to every pastor, that people have to be helped in regard to matters which the Bible takes for granted. For example, there is no attempt anywhere in the Bible to prove the existence of God. The question is one that simply does not arise. It is an accepted fact, the basic fact indeed which gives reality and meaning to everything else. The same thing is true of the validity of prayer. Jesus, for instance, nowhere makes the validity or efficacy of prayer a matter for debate. He assumes them, lives on the basis of them, interprets them to men out of a vivid, personal experience of their value and worth. The form of words preceding the Lord's Prayer is significant. It is not, "If you pray, say, Our Father," but "When you pray, say, Our Father." In preaching, however, we have to take into account men and women for whom all this is not self-evident. It is part of our duty to make faith credible, to

48

offer a reasoned justification of it, to commend it to the mind and the intelligence. To be sure, the Gospel is good news which we proclaim, but proclamation has to be supplemented by elucidation and interpretation. In the New Testament κήρυγμα and διδαχή go hand in hand. While stressing the priority of positive proclamation let us not convey the impression that there is no place in Christianity for apologetics, that it frowns upon inquiry and investigation, that it is an inscrutable revelation which none dare interrogate but which all must accept without question. Proclamation comes first, but apologetical preaching exhibits the reasonableness of belief, and seeks to promote a better understanding of what is believed.

People have to be helped also in regard to matters on which the Bible throws a flood of light. Perhaps because the bulk of my work has been done in the vicinity of college campuses I am acutely conscious of the preacher's responsibility to come to grips with the mental and moral difficulties confronting men and women in the modern world. Think of the questions they ask. Has life meaning? Does God care? Why be moral? How is one to believe in God in a world like this? Give them a chance and people ask the elemental questions. As they enlarge on them, indicating where their problems lie, what they frequently reveal is the poor caricature of Christianity which they suppose to be the authentic faith. The only Christianity they know, it turns out, is an infantile brand which is bound to make for dissatisfaction, and which is all too

49

often responsible for the nominal membership which is the glaring weakness of the Church today. It is to this type of situation, by no means confined to college campuses, that apologetical preaching can profitably address itself. Much will depend, however, not only on the intellectual strength of the case we expound but on the depth and vigor of our practical acquaintance with the religious reality underlying it.

Preaching should not be made too much an affair of argument and debate. Both are useful in removing confusion from the mind and in clearing away difficulties, but to what extent do they beget vision? Intuitive insight—Archimedes crying, "I have found it, I have found it"—everywhere precedes formal proof and so long as the insight is lacking the proof is without power to impel or constrain the mind. The lines of Omar Khayyám are familiar:

> Myself when young did eagerly frequent
> Doctor and Saint, and heard great Argument
> About it and about; but evermore
> Came out by the same door as in I went.

Matthew Arnold once affirmed that Jesus never touched theory but invariably based Himself on experience. We may often touch it but we should not major in it. Doubtless A. D. Lindsay, the Master of Balliol College, Oxford, had something of the kind in mind when, in addressing a group of ministers, he remarked about their pulpit work:

"You are arguing, and you should not argue, you should witness."

Social Preaching

In this aspect of the sermon two factors are involved. One is the combating of specific social evils—corruption and graft, juvenile and adult delinquency, drunkenness, gambling, bad housing, unfair labor practices. The pulpit is under obligation to urge Christians as citizens to come to grips with these evils and subdue them. The preacher rightly singles out for censure national sins, social injustices, racial and class prejudice, intolerance and bigotry, economic exploitation. The other factor is the drawing out of the social implications of the Gospel. The New Testament visualizes Christ as supreme in public as well as private life. There is a striking phrase in the Book of Revelation: "On His head were many crowns." What can this mean but that all the provinces of life constitute different kingdoms in which the authority of Christ is to be acknowledged and His will obeyed? As Studdert-Kennedy so well expressed it, "He is as much Lord of the mill as He is of the minster, and as much concerned with the counting house as He is with the cathedral."[2]

The contemporary situation calls clamantly for this sort of emphasis. By and large the American pulpit is much too prone to accept the political and economic limitations which secularizing influences would impose, among them

[2] *Thy Kingdom Come*, p. 99.

the dictum that whatever is economically right cannot be morally wrong. It suffers the world to draw boundaries all round the Christian religion and for the most part has been content to retire and remain within those boundaries. The demand today is for an advance into the territories from which Christianity has virtually been expelled—into politics, economics, industry, science, education, art. For our faith has to do not with a single segment of human existence but with the whole of it. The sovereignty of God extends not only over prayer and worship but over all our activities and institutions. This was the vision that came to Zechariah. "In that day shall there be on the bells of the horses, Holiness unto the Lord." Nothing in the Bible nor in the history of the Church permits us to view the Christian Faith as a purely personal concern. One of the reasons why multitudes regard it as irrelevant to the problems of everyday existence is because its accredited representatives have so little to say about the dominant social forces in economic and political life. In her autobiography, *The Long Loneliness*, Dorothy Day describes a fellow student whose conscience was disturbed about social conditions. "She never met a Christian. This I am sure is literally true. When we were at the university together, we never met anyone who had a vital faith, or, if he had one, was articulate and apostolic. There were no doubt those whose souls glowed with belief, whose hearts were warmed by the love of God, on all sides of us. But mingling as we did, in our life together, we never met any

whose personal morality was matched by a social morality
or who tried to make life here for others a foretaste of the
life to come."[3] Apposite in this context is the comment
of Christopher Dawson: "To keep religion out of public
life is to shut it up in a stuffy back drawing room with the
aspidistras and the antimacassars when the streets are full
of life and youth."[4]

Does this mean that Christian ministers should occupy
themselves in the pulpit with political and economic
questions? Many, inside and outside the çhurches, say
"No," but are they right? About such questions in their
technical aspect the average minister is not competent
to speak, but he is surely obliged to say something about
their moral aspect. It is this that makes a ministry prophetic.
To take a specific case. Bad housing is a social evil. What
changes in the economic system will best overcome it is
a technical question which experts in the field are best
qualified to answer. This does not mean, however, that a
Christian minister should say nothing about bad housing
when its evil results are obvious and glaring. It is his
responsibility to deal with its moral aspect, to show how
it blights family life, disintegrates character, makes for the
delinquency, adult and juvenile, which is currently such
a menace to the character of the nation.

In other words, it is the business of the preacher to
propound Christian principles and to point out where the

[3] Pp. 70-71.
[4] *Beyond Politics*, p. 104.

existing social order is at variance with them. His task is to stimulate the social conscience by working out the implications of the Gospel in national and international life. This may involve repercussions in the political and economic fields, for it is difficult to draw a sharp dividing line between principles of action and concrete policies. More than once it has happened that in bearing his witness on the moral aspect of social issues a minister has stirred up political controversy. Like Amos and Jeremiah ministers have been constrained to say that certain specific policies of state were a menace to the souls of the people. To the charge that this is political action the most effective rejoinder is that it is pastoral action. The prophetic denunciation of evil is involved in all faithful preaching of the Word of God. The servant of Christ is certain to find himself at odds with anything which is contrary to the good purpose of God.

There is a judicious summary of the case in Bishop Hensley Henson's autobiography. The average minister, he considers, is seldom qualified to discuss the practical questions which must be answered by the economist and the politician. "Neither his professional training nor his normal experience qualifies him for the task. He is rarely possessed either of the necessary technical knowledge or of adequate acquaintance with the relevant facts. Therefore in the pulpit he cannot wisely advance beyond a careful exposition of principles and general suggestions as to their practical expression. When, however, the facts are known, the moral principle apparent, and only their practical expression is in debate, the clergyman cannot rightly evade the responsibility which attaches to his position as a Christian teacher. He must stand forth as the official exponent and champion of Christian obligation, and at whatever cost insist, to the full extent of his opportunity, upon its fulfillment."[5]

About one thing the preacher must especially be on guard. It can be a simple matter to *denounce* social evils, particularly when preaching to people not directly implicated in them. A New England minister can let himself go about the race question; there may only be a handful of colored folk in his community. A rural Methodist minister may fulminate against the liquor traffic; none of his people may drink cocktails. Observe the Monday issues of the newspapers and note how they habitually report pulpit utterances. The descriptive verbs again and again are "chides," "raps," "scores," "hits," "blasts." We have to do more than denounce. Where social evils are concerned the vital questions have to do with cause and cure. Why do teenagers become dope addicts? What makes alcoholics, what is "eating" them? What lies back of the gambling instinct? Professing as we do to have in the Gospel a sovereign remedy for the ills of society we should concentrate on prescription as much as diagnosis; we should uncover causes and point to cures rather than engage in mere verbal vituperation.

[5] *Retrospect of an Unimportant Life*, Vol. I, p. 119.

THE MAKING OF THE SERMON

Psychological Preaching

There are some who suppose that the type of sermon which is psychological in its approach and emphasis represents a twentieth-century development. They think of Freud and Jung and their respective disciples as having opened up a whole new field for the preacher. It would be absurd to dismiss the contention. Freud's account of the Unconscious is one of the most solid gains of psychoanalysis and has radically changed our understanding of the structure of the mind. The psychologists, moreover, have made us acutely aware of the mental mechanisms of the mind—repression, projection, rationalization, compensation, phantasy; of the depth, stubbornness and evil in human nature; of the irrational and egoistic forces below the surface of human consciousness. They have demonstrated that sex is the source of much neurosis, a fact people were reluctant to acknowledge, though until it is openly acknowledged there can be no cure for certain types of neuroticism. They have shown that a traumatic experience undergone in childhood may have disastrous effects throughout the remainder of the individual's life. The impact of findings like these on Christian thought has significantly affected the character and content of present-day preaching.

It should not be forgotten, however, that while the science of psychology is modern, psychological insight is as ancient as the hills. The casebooks of psychiatrists provide the preacher with endless source material and he can make effective use of them. What he ought not to require to be told is that the supreme psychological source-book is the Bible. It is uncannily true to life, and where Freud and Jung are concerned, extraordinarily up-to-date. To neglect it and go for sermon suggestion and substance to the superficial journalistic psychology current in popular magazines is sheer dereliction of duty.

If he wants to preach about rationalization he cannot do better than turn to Elijah and the sad sequel to the triumph on Mount Carmel. The man who, singlehanded, had fearlessly confronted the prophets of Baal rose and ran for his life from the taunts and threats of a woman. Tracked down to his hiding place in the wilderness what do we find him saying? Not "I am a recreant, a coward, a poor apology for a prophet," but "I, even I only am left; and they seek my life to take it away" (I Kings 19:10). The defense mechanism is at work. He is making an alibi do duty for self-blame. Where could one secure a more telling illustration of rationalization? His mind has arrived at a compromise which will give it a measure of peace. He is not *deliberately* manufacturing an excuse to save his feelings. He cannot be charged with conscious hypocrisy. He is evading the facts but he is unconscious of evading them. This is what makes rationalization so mischievous. Elijah is emphasizing a fact—his solitariness in Israel, though he is not nearly as solitary as he supposes—but it is obscuring the true fact, that he has shirked his duty, deserted his post, been frightened out of his wits by Jezebel. And the contemporary application? What we call our conscious mind is only a small part of our total mind. Underneath the self-conscious processes of thought and will are the unconscious processes, obscurely motivated passions and prejudices, illusions and delusions, likes and dislikes. It is not a simple matter to put a finger on the ugly facts about ourselves. They slip so easily into the unconscious. We are such born rationalizers.

Or, if the preacher, seeing the mischief wrought by the mechanism of the mind called repression, wants to preach about it, he has a perfect example in the life story of David (II Sam. 11:2-12:7). What David did in the matter of the wife of Uriah, the Hittite, was dastardly. He not only took Bathsheba from Uriah, but put him in the front line of battle so that he was killed. Yet when the prophet Nathan went and told David the story of the rich man with many flocks and herds who took the poor man's one ewe lamb, he was passionately indignant with the rich man and there and then condemned him to death. It never occurred to him, until Nathan courageously blurted out, "Thou art the man," that it was his own shameful behavior he was condemning. He had repressed the memory of it and the guilt of it. Memory and guilt alike had sunk into his unconscious where they were not dead and done with but festering and ulcerating. He gained a measure of relief by projection, being angry with his own fault when he saw it in someone else. What a defense mechanism—condemning in others what we refuse to admit in ourselves!

Or, take the emphasis placed by psychologists on the need for self-acceptance. They have proved that much of the hypertension, neurasthenia, neurosis of our time comes from the failure of people to live happily and harmoniously with themselves. We have got to be at rights with ourselves, but the only way to be that is to face the facts about ourselves. Alibis, evasions, rationalizations—they are all mischief-makers. Once again the Bible offers an unforgettable illustration, that of Jacob at Peniel (Gen. 32:24 ff.). He had tricked his father Isaac, his brother Esau, his uncle Laban, and as a result of unscrupulous dealing was a prosperous man. But—just like John P. Marquand's Willis Wayde—he had never stopped long enough to take a good look at himself. He had been running away from himself for a long time. At Peniel he had it out with himself. "What kind of man am I? What is my real character?" He wrestled all night with something devilish in himself, and after an agonizing struggle he faced the ugly facts about himself. "I am Jacob—a twister." And it was then, evasions done with, disguises cast aside, that he became a new man, "No more Jacob but Israel—a prince with God."

While talking not long ago with a psychiatrist I saw a Bible on his desk. When I referred to it he told me that it was in his hands every day. He had learned what many a minister has still to realize, and realizing to work out in his preaching, that the soundest and shrewdest psychology is to be found in the Bible.

Evangelical Preaching

Perhaps this can best be described as preaching for a verdict. When in my first charge, a member of the church who was a lawyer, induced me to spend a day with him at the courts. The big occasion of the day was the impassioned plea made by counsel for the defense in a murder trial. On the way home, reverting to the speech that had held us spellbound, my friend said, "He was out for a verdict and bent on getting it. You preachers fill the same role, don't you?" He set me thinking. Had I been preaching for a verdict? In how many sermons had I aimed at securing whole-souled commitment to Jesus Christ? That day in the courts, and the pointed query in the conversation that followed it, gave a new emphasis to my preaching. It helped me to appreciate that the Word of God should be proclaimed so as to result in a personal encounter.

The preacher as evangelist stands in the pulpit not chiefly as a disseminator of ideas but as one charged with responsibility for confronting his hearers with God. The religion he seeks to advance is not first and foremost a religion of ideas but the religion of a Person. His consuming concern is not to secure intellectual assent to a number of ethical and theological propositions but to bring about a face-to-face meeting with Jesus Christ. What George Eliot wrote about ideals applies equally to ideas: they are poor ghosts until they become incarnate. It requires more than intellectual assent to the ideas, or ideals, of goodness, truth and righteousness to make a character and save a soul. Matthew Arnold summed the matter up when he said, "A correct, scientific statement of rules of virtue has upon the great majority of mankind simply no effect at all." In the New Testament nobody is concerned to provide a correct, scientific statement of rules of virtue. There the beginning and the end of preaching is to pave the way to a personal encounter with God in Christ.

It is impressive to note how of late one thinker after another—Barth (deriving the original stimulus from Kierkegaard), Heim, Brunner, John Baillie, John A. Mackay, H. H. Farmer—has insisted on the crucial importance in religion of this personal encounter. Farmer has carefully wrought out its relation to preaching in his book *The Servant of the Word*.[6] God, he maintains, never enters into personal relationship with a man apart from other human persons. The spoken word is right at the center of the I-Thou relationship, and the written or printed word is therefore always a poor substitute for it. In every true sermon there is a direct and personal encounter—a meeting of mind with mind, personality with personality, will with will. It has always something of the directness of Nathan's word to David, "Thou art the man!" The preacher must always be out for a verdict in the mind of his hearers so profound that both feeling and will are involved, a

[6] Pp. 40 ff.

verdict such as disposes them individually to say, "Now it is in my heart to make a covenant with the Lord."

Life-Situation Preaching

In all this there has been no mention of life-situation preaching, the type commonest today in the United States. Seeking to avoid the remoteness and irrelevance, not to say unreality, which are the bane of much biblical exposition, it starts with people where they are, which was what Jesus did over and over again. The point of departure is a live issue of some kind. It may be personal or social; it may be theological or ethical. Whatever it is, the preacher makes it his business to get at the core of the problem, and, that done, he goes on to work out the solution, with the biblical revelation, and the mind and spirit of Christ, as the constant points of reference and direction.

Life-situation preaching is often criticized because the temptation besetting many who specialize in it is that they become wholly preoccupied with issues of the hour. This is what accounts for the secular and indeed shallow aspect of much contemporary preaching. Its primary sources are the newspaper, the weekly magazines, the digests, and only secondarily the Word of God. What is said in church on Sunday frequently has the character of editorial comment with a mild religious flavor. It lacks any distinctive Christian insight and emphasis. Evidence is not wanting that these weaknesses are more and more being recognized and corrected.

62

Dr. Fosdick is the outstanding advocate of life-situation preaching, and in the judgment of many its greatest exponent. In July, 1928, he contributed an article to *Harper's Magazine* entitled "What Is the Matter with Preaching?" Wherever we put the stress in our work in the pulpit, the article has a paragraph we do well to ponder. It describes the situation when we stand up to preach. "Those men and women in front of you are nearly all facing problems. One woman has begun a dangerous liaison with a married man. That widow is seething with resentment because her only son wants to get married. That man works for an irate boss who expects him to lie for him on occasion. That girl is smouldering with sex and has begun to think that her past firmness in moral conviction is only prudery and that she will miss her chance of being wed unless she is more free with boys. . . . A problem in nearly every pew. Face them! Face them one by one! Start your sermon by sketching the problem. It is not a theoretical problem. It is practical, living, urgent. That is where people want your help. Even when you are dealing with a problem that is not his own, every man will feel the thrust of your words upon some one else, and will long for the answer. Bring preaching close to life. That is the urgent need today. Nothing so much as this would make the pulpit powerful once more."

Yes, whether expository, ethical, devotional, theological, apologetical, social, psychological, evangelical, topical, bring preaching close to life.

63

Preaching As An Art

❦

I t is in many ways strange that I should be delivering this
particular series of lectures. I attended a divinity school
which had no department of Homiletics. In the space of
three years I heard only four lectures in Pastoral Theology,
delivered by a parish minister, and they had to do with the
conduct of marriages and funerals and the cure of souls
in general. There was not a word about the making of the
sermon. Since then the establishment of the Warrack Lectures has meant that in the four Scottish Divinity Schools
students at least have an opportunity in alternate years of
hearing journeyman ministers deal with some aspect of the
preaching office.

I hasten to add that one of the professors digressed at
intervals to offer comments bearing on the fact that the men
in his class would in all likelihood spend a not inconsider-
able portion of their time preparing sermons. Some of
his asides linger in the memory. "Strike the nail on the
head, but don't split the wood." "Avoid the clamorous pre-
sentation of the obvious." "Don't call a man deep when

he is muddy." "Love simple speech as much as you hate shallow thinking." "If you haven't struck oil in five minutes, stop boring." There was another professor who delivered himself one morning of the dictum, "It takes an extraordinary concatenation of meteorological circumstances to induce some people to go to church." Much more to the point was the comment of a Scottish beadle (church caretaker) I knew. Discussing the vagaries of churchgoers, he said, "If it's wet they'll no' come out; and if it's dry they'll no' come in."

Most of my contemporaries on graduating became assistants to ministers. To begin with they were responsible only for occasional preaching but they were in close, everyday association with an experienced practitioner. They had ample opportunities of observing him at work—his management of his week, the nature and scope of his reading, his technique in preparing and delivering his sermons. The senior minister for the most part was ready enough to counsel and advise. Such private tutoring may not have compensated for the absence of a homiletics course but it had very genuine values. Men who assisted Alexander Whyte or George Morrison or Norman MacLean acquired a liberal education in every aspect of the work of the ministry.

Two considerations suggest themselves in this regard. The first is that none of us should hesitate to pick the brains of older preachers. We can pay them no higher compliment than to ask them how they go about their work.

It surprises me that it is not done more frequently. There never was a preacher yet of average ability from whom a fellow craftsman could not learn something.

I remember in 1937 finding myself in a three-day association with F. W. Norwood, who was then minister of the City Temple, London. I had always been fascinated by and envious of one feature of his preaching, its completely extemporaneous character. He used no notes, excepting for a few slips of paper consisting of quotations, and as a rule very few of those. Yet he managed to do what so many extemporaneous preachers fail to do; he avoided repetition of phraseology, there was no overworking of words, his style was not only natural and engaging but vital and vigorous.

I asked him for his secret. He said there was no secret, only a method experimented with over a long term of years and adhered to thereafter because it had proved the most serviceable method for him. Norwood told me that once he had fixed on a subject he would lie down on a sofa and let his mind go to work on the subject. One by one ideas would suggest themselves to him and he would proceed to sort them out in sequence. Gradually the sermon outline would begin to take form. When I indicated that the sofa might incline some to undue relaxation, if not woolgathering or worse, he insisted that what was involved for him was the strictest concentration and mental activity. It was his contention that if ideas are clear in the mind, and a man has reasonable facility of speech, he will have no problem in the matter of expression. He will have no need even to jot down heads or divisions. The structure and sequence will stand out in the memory.

This, obviously, is not a method for every man. I have tried it, and for a time made a special point of persisting with it, but only with limited success. I have discovered that Norwood is right about one important particular: if ideas are clearly envisaged and retained in the mind there is no problem of expression. The words flow and they match the thoughts. It is incontestable that a great deal of slipshod speaking is due primarily to fuzzy thinking. The soldier, moreover, had a point when he remarked to his chaplain, who had leaned hard on his manuscript in delivering his sermon: "How do you expect us to remember it, Padre, when you don't remember it yourself?" The logic of that is unassailable.

On the other hand, if you were to ask Dr. Fosdick about his techniques in preaching you would be introduced to a method as dissimilar to Dr. Norwood's as it well could be. For years now Dr. Fosdick has written every word of his sermons. He has labored long and arduously over the writing of them—polishing phrases, sentences, paragraphs; spending several mornings over one sermon; then taking the finished product with him into the pulpit, where because so much work has been done on it there is never any question of addiction to it or of reading it slavishly; it can be preached freely and vigorously and with every indication of spontaneity.

The techniques of preaching are numerous. I have indicated two that are in pronounced contrast. It is for every man by constant experimentation, by the trial-and-error approach, to discover what is the most effective method for him. And because to the day of his retirement he should be seeking to improve and perfect his preaching there is every reason why he should ask others how they go about the sermon-making art.

The second consideration suggested by the Divinity School experience is that we should not rely too much on techniques. The "know how" is important but it is not everything. There is point to the old saying that preachers are born not made. The really indispensable qualification is the preaching instinct. Some men can see possibilities in a text or topic at once; others require to have all the germinal thinking done for them. Originality and creativity in preaching seem in case after case to be a matter of native endowment. The seminary may stimulate them. I doubt whether it can impart them. Lectures in Homiletics do not account for the preaching genius of F. W. Robertson or Phillips Brooks or James S. Stewart. But one cannot fail to observe how the native endowment is nourished and sustained by a faith, first hand and vital, in Christ and His Gospel, by a love of truth and a passion for righteousness. Without these the best techniques we can devise and improvise are of little avail.

Preachers are born and not made, but they are born raw. It is invariably the case that powerful preaching represents an achievement behind which there lies an infinite capacity for taking pains. The biographies of the great personalities of the pulpit all tell the same story, a story of dedication and discipline, of men who toiled unremittingly at their task, never taking their skills for granted but endeavoring year after year to raise the standard and quality of their work. Aren't the ablest preachers you know men whose application and industry are limitless? I find them jealous of their study hours, keen in their intellectual interests, making an attempt to be wide in their reading, taking endless pains over their sermons, and ceaselessly on the lookout for anything that will make them more effective.

We should not set too much store by preaching techniques, but we cannot afford to be indifferent to them. The primary thing is the preaching instinct. Without some semblance of it at the outset there is reason to doubt whether a man should enter the ministry at all. The more marked the native gift, however, the less justification there is for trading on it. In all the denominations there are ministers, fluent in speech, not without the ability to think freshly and creatively, with more than a homiletical knack, who have never fulfilled the promise of their seminary days, and now never will, because being masters of their own time they have not disciplined themselves to budget it, but have grown slack and indolent and rarely tax themselves to excel in their work.

Half the battle is fought if we think of preaching as an art and of ourselves as artists. It is salutary to reflect how others toil over their craft. On alternate Friday afternoons

I go to Carnegie Hall to hear the New York Philharmonic Symphony Orchestra conducted by Dimitri Mitropoulos. I find in the experience a stimulus for duty on Sunday. It is not only the kindling, inspirational quality of the music, it is the discipline incarnate in the conductor. He rarely has a score before him when he steps onto the podium. He is completely the master of his materials and has his orchestra sensitive to his every wish. He is a dedicated personality; his body, mind and spirit are wholly given over to his art. To watch him is to be rebuked and challenged to higher standards of preparation and consecration. If we applied ourselves as assiduously to our craft as Mitropoulos does to his, our people might be at a loss to account for the change that would come over our preaching, but how they would welcome it!

J. H. Jowett in his Yale Lectures, *The Preacher, His Life and Work,* out of his personal experience offered this counsel. "Be as systematic as a business man. Enter your study at an appointed hour, and let that hour be as early as the earliest of your business men goes to his warehouse or his office. I remember in my earlier days how I used to hear the factory operatives passing my house on the way to the mills, where work began at six o'clock. I can recall the sound of their iron-clogs ringing through the street. The sound of the clogs fetched me out of bed and took me to my work. I no longer hear the Yorkshire clogs, but I can see and hear my business men as they start off early to earn their daily bread. And shall their minister be behind them in his quest of the Bread of Life? Shall he slouch and loiter into the day, shamed by those he assumes to lead, and shall his indolence be obtrusive in the services of the sanctuary when 'the hungry sheep look up and are not fed'? Let the minister, I say, be as businesslike as the business man."[1]

As even a casual glance at any of his books of sermons will demonstrate, Jowett, too, was a disciplined and dedicated craftsman. He used to say that preaching that costs nothing will accomplish nothing, and that if the study is a lounge the pulpit will be an impertinence. What an offense to both God and man a careless, slipshod, ill-wrought sermon is! Hard put to it to conceal his impatience with preaching of the easygoing, casual, ungirt kind, a parishioner with a biting tongue let drop the remark, "The miracle of miracles is the survival of the Church." There are preachers whose work is done in lamentably pedestrian fashion, who never stretch themselves in their preparation for the pulpit, to whom apparently it seldom or never occurs that preaching is an art and that they are artists. Other arts a man may master in a lifetime, but this does not happen to be one of them. About preaching it is men like Jowett who are the first to say, *Ars longa, vita brevis*.

Because preaching is an art there is every reason why the entire sermon should be written in full. This rule should obtain no matter how the sermon is delivered, whether extemporaneously, from notes copious or brief, or with the complete manuscript under eye. Some preachers,

[1] P. 116.

perhaps the majority, dispense with writing. In nine cases out of ten the wisdom of this may well be doubted. I have in my possession an original Charles Haddon Spurgeon sermon manuscript. It consists of a single sheet of paper, about four inches broad and seven inches long. The sermon—numbered 3270!—was an exposition of the first Psalm. The notation is as follows:

Psalm i

I. The Blessed man—
What he avoids—
What he delights in—
What he does—
Wherein he is blessed.
Who is his guardian.
II. The Cursed man

Only men of quite exceptional talent should venture with such slender equipment into the pulpit. A Spurgeon could do it but we should not too quickly assume that we are as richly endowed in power of thought or in readiness of utterance as he manifestly was when he preached the sermon numbered 3270. I keep filed with the original Spurgeon manuscript a facsimile of a portion of another sermon, printed after he had preached it, and showing his proof corrections. There are almost forty emendations on one page, all of them indicating how scrupulous Spurgeon was about considerations of style.

If only as a discipline we should write our sermons. To

do so will help us to avoid what is the bane of much extemporaneous preaching, prolixity, discursiveness, the overworking of words, the repetition of phrases. Indeed, it is when we write steadily week by week that we really begin to notice how the use of adverbs and adjectives can be overdone, how as we begin new paragraphs we have to teach ourselves to vary both the approach and the mode of expression, and especially how hard we must work to be free from ambiguity and to make our meaning crystal clear.

I question whether anything like justice has been done to the value of *style* in preaching. Sir Walter Moberly relates how at an educational conference a hard-bitten pagan administrator heard a divine speak in the traditional language of Christian devotion and was so bored and alienated that he barely restrained himself from walking out. But then there followed another representative of the churches who spoke in terse, vivid, forthright language. The administrator listened with keen interest. At the end he whispered to his neighbor, "You know, I could talk to that man. We might not agree but I could talk to him."[2] A real contact had been established, where before there was none. Style is a factor in the person-to-person encounter at which preaching aims.

There are people who are word-deaf just as some are color-blind. It is a misfortune when a preacher has no feeling for the magic of words and no flair for word-weaving. We should care for words, should select them judiciously

[2] *The Crisis in the University*, p. 117.

73

and lovingly. Barrie said about Stevenson, "He plays upon words as if they were a musical instrument." The fact of the matter is that most of us do our writing and speaking in clichés, in trite, hackneyed and stereotyped phrases. We should cultivate the sense of the sound, value and association of words, of individual words. The truth merits the noblest expression we can give it. A well-constructed sentence makes the thought it conveys lucid and adds to its persuasiveness.

My contention here is borne out by the testimony of Willard L. Sperry in a fascinating chapter contributed to *Thirteen Americans: Their Spiritual Autobiographies.* "The only technical homiletical discipline to which I have consciously and conscientiously stuck is the endeavor to learn how to handle words. They are so elusive and deceptive. They are such an imperfect medium for self-expression and are so often misinterpreted. But one of my secret and imperfectly realized ideals is that, somehow, I might be able to make words obey, to make them come to heel, as Milton and Wordsworth have done in their sonnets. The problem there is, of course, not that of the words themselves, but of the ideas behind the words. But I still maintain that a preacher in a pulpit ought to be able to handle the English language with decent competence."[3]

It is possible, to be sure, to pay too much attention to style, and the consequences then are apt to be disastrous. Where there is an excessive air of deliberation speaking and

[3] P. 251.

writing both suffer. The hallmark of a good style is that it leaves the impression that it is executed effortlessly and with ease, though in point of fact it may be the product of constant effort and striving. As for daintiness of diction, it conveys an impression of effeminacy. Language that is over-studied and overelaborated may turn out to be "faultily faultless, icily regular, splendidly null." Worse, if any-thing, than daintiness of diction is magniloquence, the repeated use of stately and high-sounding phrases that may mean nothing in particular. Not uncommonly this is matched either by obscurity or poverty of thought. John Buchan· has a story indicating that this was the fate that befell Lord Haldane. At a certain election he was defend-ing Lord Milner's policy of Chinese labor on the Rand in South Africa before a Scottish Border audience. Buchan came out of the hall with two old farmers and overheard one of them say in bewilderment to his neighbor, "Was he for it or against it?" "Ah'm damned if ah ken," was the reply. At one of his meetings Dick Sheppard heard a young minister pray, "O Lord, reveal Thyself to us in all Thine eschatological glory." His comment afterwards was, "God, who made me simple, make me simpler yet." In the House of Commons Ramsay Macdonald was once making a lengthy speech, the language grandiose, the thought com-plicated and clouded, when Winston Churchill rose, and pointing a finger at his opponent, exclaimed, "The Boneless Wonder!"

Much as Barrie admired Stevenson's style he said about

him: "He will have to take existence more seriously, to weave broadcloth instead of lace." In his later work Stevenson did just that. The style is more vigorous, incisive and direct. The words are more vivid, robust, abrupt. Right to the last Stevenson kept on cultivating an ear for the value of words. We ought to do no less. We should avoid as we would the plague flatness, dullness, clichés, the fatuities of commonplace speech. Let no one say ironically about our preaching, "Give us this day our daily platitude."

In all this Jesus is our Exemplar. What a master of speech He was! He must surely have cultivated an ear for the music and value of words. The parable of the Prodigal Son will serve as an illustration—perfect in phrasing, without a superfluous word, thought and language ideally matched. In 1768, gilding the lily if ever anyone did, a clergyman named Harwood rendered the opening sentence of the parable thus: "A Gentleman of a splendid family and opulent fortune had two sons." This was how he expressed the prodigal's resolve when in the far country: "I am determined to go to my dear aged parent, and try to excite his tenderness and compassion for me—I will kneel before him and accost him in these penitent and pathetic terms.—Best of parents! I acknowledge myself an ungrateful creature to heaven and to you!"[4] By comparison the speech of Jesus is simple, lucid, terse. If the common people heard Him gladly, went away after hearing Him saying, "Never man spake like this man," and, "He

[4] Quoted in John Oman, *Concerning the Ministry*, p. 124.

speaks with authority and not like our clergy," it was partly because His speech was crystal clear, noble truth matched by noble expression.

I know of no one who has brought this out more convincingly than T. R. Glover in *The Jesus of History,* and I shall quote him at some length in concluding this lecture. "Look at His method of teaching. People 'marvelled at His words of charm' (Luke 4:22)—'hung about Him to hear Him' (Luke 19:48). He said that the word is the overflow of the heart. 'Out of the abundance of the heart the mouth speaketh' (Matt. 12:34; Luke 6:45). What a heart, then, His words reveal! How easy and straightforward His language is! Today we all use abstract nouns to convey our meaning; we cannot do without words ending in -ality and -ation. But there is no recorded saying of Jesus where He even uses 'personality.' He does not use abstract nouns. He sticks to plain words. When He speaks about God He does not say 'the great First Cause,' or 'Providence,' or any other vague abstract. Still less does He use an adverb from the abstract, like 'providentially.' He says 'your heavenly Father.' He does not talk of 'humanity'; He says 'your brethren.'

"With this remark His own gift of arresting phrase; the freshness of His language, how free it is from quotation, how natural and how extraordinarily simple. Everything worth while can be put in simple language; and if the speech is complicated, it is a call to think again. 'As a woman over-curiously trimmed is to be mistrusted, so is a

F 77

speech,' said John Robinson of Leyden, the minister of the Pilgrim Fathers. The language of Jesus is simple and direct, the inevitable expression of a rich nature and a habit of truth. You feel He does not strain after effect—epigram, antithesis or alliteration. Of course, He uses such things —like all real speakers—but He does not go out of His way for them. No, and so much the more significant are such characteristic antitheses as: 'Ye cannot serve God and Mammon' (Luke 6:13), and 'Whosoever will save his life shall lose it' (Matt. 16:25), coming with a spontaneous flash, and answering in their sharpness to the sharp edges of fact. His words caught the attention, and lived in the memory; they revealed such a nature; they were so living and unforgettable."[5]

There, Gentlemen, is our model, and what a perfect model it is!

[5] Pp. 83-85.

The Construction of the Sermon

Since style is an integral and indispensable element in effective preaching some consideration should be given to its cultivation. It can best be acquired by tireless industry and application *in writing*. Genius in this field, as in any other, is an infinite capacity for taking pains. Authors of distinction, in describing how their works are produced, with extraordinary unanimity tell the same story; they toil incessantly. When Boswell inquired of Dr. Johnson how it came about that even in casual conversation he never fell below a finished stateliness of expression, the answer was that he had early resolved never to write or speak except with his loins girt.

If Johnson and the eighteenth century seem remote the case of Somerset Maugham may be cited. In *The Summing Up*, which if not an autobiography is full of candid self-revelation, and a book particularly to be read by ministers because of its provocative observations on men, manners and morals, a great deal is said about style. This, for example. "A good style should show no sign of effort. What is written should seem a happy accident. I think no one in France now writes more admirably than Colette, and such is the ease of her expression that you cannot bring yourself to believe that she takes any trouble over it. I am told that there are pianists who have a natural technique so that they can play in a manner that most executants can achieve only as the result of unremitting toil, and I am willing to believe that there are writers who are equally fortunate. Among them I was much inclined to place Colette. I asked her. I was exceedingly surprised to hear that she wrote everything over and over again. She told me that she would often spend a whole morning working upon a single page. But it does not matter how one gets the effect of ease. For my part, if I get it at all, it is only by strenuous effort. Nature seldom provides me with the word, the turn of phrase, that is appropriate without being far-fetched or commonplace."[1]

Style is acquired by *intensive reading* as well as by industry in writing. It is nourished by steeping the mind in the great masterpieces of literature. Foremost among these is the King James Version of the Bible. For rich and glorious Anglo-Saxon English it is unsurpassed. Be sure to study what John Ruskin has to say about this in *Sesame and Lilies,* and the perceptive comments of Arthur Quiller Couch in *The Art of Reading.* The element of style is vital just because the expression adds immeasurably to the power with which the subject matter appeals to us. Take, for

[1] P. 30.

instance, the psalm which affirms so movingly the omnipresence of God. "Whither shall I go from Thy Spirit?
or whither shall I flee from Thy presence? If I ascend up
into heaven, Thou art there: if I make my bed in hell,
behold, Thou art there. If I take the wings of the morning,
and dwell in the uttermost parts of the sea; even there shall
Thy hand lead me, and Thy right hand shall hold me. If
I say, Surely the darkness shall cover me; even the night
shall be light about me. Yea, the darkness hideth not from
Thee; but the night shineth as the day: the darkness and
the light are both alike to Thee" (Ps. 139:7-12). There
are passages innumerable in Scripture whose spell over
us would be broken were they to be so rewritten that
while the ideas remained the same the expression was
changed into pedestrian prose. One Sunday Alexander
Whyte, after reading as the Scripture for the day Psalm
103, omitted the customary formula, "Here endeth the
Old Testament lesson," and substituted for it the exclamation, "If Shakespeare had written it we should never have
heard the end of it." Who can estimate the formative influence on style and eloquence—I am not talking about
oratory—exercised by the Bible?

Poetry also nourishes style. To read it is to get into
the habit of looking intensely at words. Unless we are word-
deaf it inclines us to select words judiciously and lovingly.
The poets have a keener insight into the real significance
of things than most of us. This is why we call them seers
—they see further and deeper than the rest of us. They are

able to use language in such wonderful fashion as to conjure up for us a sense of beauty or power, the existence of which we had not suspected, or only vaguely at the back of our minds. Inspiration comes largely from keeping company with the inspired. The expression of such inspiration as we have will come better by the unconscious influence of example—the example of Shakespeare, Wordsworth, Browning, Yeats, Whitman, Frost—than by self-conscious effort after an eloquent style.

I am tempted to speak at some length about reading in general. Books are the preacher's tools. John Oman ventured the opinion that no one has ever been a great speaker who was not an omnivorous reader.[2] As a rule, the caliber of a minister can be judged by his library. Excepting for his public prayers nothing about him is so self-revealing. I heard about a member of a pulpit committee who went to hear a candidate preach. The candidate invited him to dinner at the manse. The visitor was appalled by the location and size of the study. It was one of the pokiest rooms in the house, there were less than two hundred books on the shelves, and those that were religious were mostly books of sermons.

Reading can be overdone. There are sermons that are too bookish. They suggest that the preacher knows more about literature than about life and that he is talking about things at second hand. They prompt the question, "Sayest thou this thing of thyself, or did others tell it thee of me?" (John

[2] *Op. cit.*, p. 164.

18:34). Sermons replete with quotations from poets, novel-
ists, philosophers, scientists may afford more satisfaction
to the man in the pulpit than to his hearers in the pew,
who may be of the opinion that the discourse to which they
are listening lacks a down-to-earth quality. But with the
rush and pace of life what they are, and with the demands
on ministers so multifarious and insistent, few of us are
likely to read too much or to overdo quotations, at any
rate directly, from literary sources. I emphasize the adverb
directly because some who are resourceful in the use of
books of quotations come by a reputation for a wide knowledge of literature to which in actuality they have no claim.
The likelihood is that we shall have to fight hard and
long to make and keep a place for steady and substantial
reading—one really difficult book always stretching our
mind and others fertilizing and nourishing it.

As to the type of books to be read, the important thing
is to keep one's reading comprehensive. Even so, every man
is likely to gravitate to some special field or fields, not only
because of personal inclination but because of what he dis-
covers it yields in homiletical provocation and suggestion.
By and large, the reading for the pulpit which for me is
most rewarding is biography and autobiography. A ministerial acquaintance who budgets his time scrupulously, tells
me that he varies his reading—poetry for style, history for
perspective, philosophy for depth, science for objectivity,
current literature to maintain close contact with everyday affairs. It is an ambitious pattern, and one that the

THE MAKING OF THE SERMON

average minister would find it difficult to adhere to, but it is better to have an ambitious pattern and fall short of it than to have no pattern at all.

The reference to current literature prompts an observation about the newspaper. It will not do to skim it through, for we ought not to be intellectual aliens, like preachers of a former generation who were said to be "invisible all week and incomprehensible on Sunday." We should know what is going on in our community and in the larger world. If we are to speak to our generation we shall require to have a finger on its pulse. For all that, the newspaper should never have pride of place with us, nor is there any justification for giving it, as is the settled habit of some, the best hours of the morning. This applies also to periodicals and magazines. They serve to keep us in touch with current events and to provide our thinking with stimulus and substance, but they should be selected with discrimination and kept, as to the time they consume, within strict limits. They should not be permitted to become the staple feature of our mental diet. Some ministers who never read a big or demanding book in a year peruse an inordinate amount of ephemeral literature, and the results are only too dismally apparent in the shallow topicality of their preaching. Said Ruskin, "Do you know, if you read this, that you cannot read that—that what you lose today you cannot gain tomorrow?"[3] It was Ruskin, too, who inquired with indignation, "What! And do your priests not know their sacred

[3] *Op. cit.*, p. 19.

books?" He meant the Old Testament and the New Testament in the original! He would have been provoked by seminaries which do not even require Greek from candidates for the ministry.

What about books of sermons as a homiletical source? "At all costs avoid them," some say, having in mind the plagiarizing tendency. A gifted Scottish preacher told me that he dared not look at any sermon preached by Maclaren of Manchester on a text on which he was working. It was his unvarying experience that his judgment bowed down before Maclaren's so that he saw in the text only what Maclaren saw, and inclined not only to the same general outline but even to the same divisions and subdivisions. This is what is bound to happen, no matter who is the author of the book of sermons—Fosdick, Stewart, Weatherhead, Sockman—if the volume is consulted on Friday night or Saturday morning, and the sermon still has to be prepared. There is no time then for original, reflective, creative work. Books of sermons should be consulted, but for purposes of study. They should serve as models, as illustrations of the way in which others go about the craft of sermon-making—the character of the texts and topics they select; what they do with them; whether they take one idea and develop and elaborate it, or take several ideas and work with divisions and subdivisions; their use of illustrations and the nature of them.

The point was made earlier that there are preachers who leave the impression that their knowledge of life and of the human heart is a bookish knowledge; it has an academic flavor, an abstract, speculative quality. Do you recall Kipling's description of Tomlinson's encounter with Peter at the gate of heaven?

> "Stand up, stand up now, Tomlinson, and answer
> loud and high
> The good that ye did for the sake of men or
> ever ye came to die—
> The good that ye did for the sake of men in the
> little earth so lone!"
> And the naked soul of Tomlinson grew white as
> a rain-washed bone. . . .
> "This I have read in a book," he said, "and
> that was told to me,
> And this I have thought that another man thought
> of a Prince in Muscovy."
> The good souls flocked like homing doves
> and bade him clear the path,
> And Peter twirled the jangling keys in
> weariness and wrath.
> "Ye have read, ye have heard, ye have thought,"
> he said, "and the tale is yet to run:
> By the worth of the body that once ye had,
> give answer—what ha' ye done?"[4]

Keep your reading wide, but never forget that the school of experience is a fruitful, long-term source for the preacher.

[4] "Tomlinson" from *Departmental Ditties and Ballads and Barrack-Room Ballads*, by Rudyard Kipling. Reprinted by permission of Mrs. George Bambridge, Doubleday & Company, Inc., and The Macmillan Co. of Canada.

What goes on in us and around us should keep us plentifully supplied with sermon substance. Alexander Whyte sent a letter of congratulation to one of his assistants when his first child was born. "This child," he wrote, "will teach you more than did all your professors." There are great preachers who are omnivorous readers but whose knowledge of men and character comes out of life as well as literature, comes out of firsthand observation and an everyday sharing of the life of the people to whom they preach. A good pastor is not necessarily a great preacher, but he is almost certain to be a helpful preacher if he learns to turn to account his unique opportunities of observing human nature at close quarters, in all its variety of mood and temper, in all its strangely mingled strength and weakness, big and yet so little, lovable and yet so chronically self-centered, at once a son of Adam and a son of God. A man sat in a minister's study repeating over and over again, "How could I have done it? How could I have done it?" Which was the true man, the perpetrator of a shameful wrong, or the conscience-stricken individual wringing his hands and genuinely lamenting his offense? Pondering that, the minister in question went back to Romans 7 with a new awareness of its pathos and poignancy.

Nevertheless, there are dangers here. There is the type of man who draws far too heavily on personal experience, his own experience. He makes prodigal use of the first personal pronoun (which Edward Gibbon described as the most indecent of all the pronouns), and has his long-suffering congregation familiar to the point of weariness with his own and his family's doings. I remember how during the first world war a minister in our town went off to France to serve with the Y.M.C.A. How his congregation lived to regret that six months! For long enough afterwards his sermons were interlarded with anecdotes which began, "When I was in France . . ." In all the situations depicted, too, he seemed to be at the center of things, filling a role of importance and leadership such as we never knew him to fill at home.

There is another danger. When drawing on pastoral experience, we have to be on our guard against anything that even remotely involves a breach of confidence. What is told us as counselors should not be retailed afterwards for public consumption. Nothing will so undermine the faith of our people in us as their discovery that we cannot be relied upon to keep to ourselves information that has been given to us in what is virtually the confessional. The complexion of the case is altered when a man asks, as Leslie Weatherhead indicates he regularly does, whether he may make an anonymous, impersonal use from the pulpit of an experience in which he has been involved as confidant and counselor.

As for the art of constructing a specific sermon, for what it is worth and at the risk of overworking the most indecent of all the pronouns, I shall say something about the method I follow. I need to know by Monday morning at the latest what the subject and title are to be for the following Sunday. These are required for the bulletin board, the church calendar and the press. Incidentally, I can never quite make out why some ministers are so dilatory in keeping their bulletin boards up-to-date. Some time ago in a university town, with the church adjoining the campus, I saw the title of the minister's sermon of the previous Sunday remain on the bulletin board all through the week; it was only taken down at noon on the Saturday. Judge for yourself what an alert and wide-awake student would think of such indolence. It may be remarked in the bygoing that the choice of a title is no small task. It may repel as much as it attracts. Pertinent enough in itself it may not prove inviting to the majority. I notice that when I preach on "What To Do with Our Fears" the request for copies of the sermon is greater than when the theme is "The Christian View of History." Yet it is surely as much the duty of the preacher to deal with the latter subject as with the former.

The Monday date line means that my mind is working consciously and subconsciously on the subject all week. Though selected on Monday, I make a start on the preparation of the sermon on Tuesday morning. Whyte, who was in his study at nine on Mondays, was as a rule free from preparation by Saturday at midday, and would spend the afternoon in walking, and the evening with magazines and periodicals. I doubt whether many ministers nowadays, with institutional work so demanding, could follow such a schedule. Most require Monday off, at least from sermon-making, though not necessarily from all work.

On Tuesday morning I begin to sift out and systematize my source materials. These I assemble in a large notebook, the texts with a double page each in one half of the book, the subjects with a double page each in the other half. I rarely write a sermon "from scratch" or under the inspiration of the moment. If the source materials are extensive, and having accumulated over a period of time they usually are, the sifting process may be a quite lengthy one. Not infrequently it involves a good deal of reading. A reference to an author means consulting the specific page, and that in turn may carry one on from page to page. But it is early in the week and there is no need for haste and no sense of pressure. Always, when working with a text, the original has to be consulted and the commentaries. Commentaries in a complete series are liable to be unequal. For the most part, it is wise to buy them singly, not in a complete set. Some I find invaluable—Marcus Dods on Genesis, George Adam Smith on Isaiah, C. H. Dodd on Romans, J. M. E. Ross on the First Epistle of Peter, W. M. Macgregor on the Epistle to the Galatians, John Mackay on the Epistle to the Ephesians.

The sifting process completed, I begin to sketch an outline. At the start this is merely tentative and experimental. The first draft is almost certain to find its way to the wastepaper basket as improvements, adjustments and alterations commend themselves. As the outline gradu-

ally takes shape I work the source material into it—
quotations, incidents, illustrations. Usually I spend the
whole of Tuesday morning on this assignment. By noon
both outline and general content are decided upon. The
sermon is then well on its way. To know where you are
going by noon on Tuesday is to take to the street, to
your pastoral visitation and community and committee
labors, without pulpit forebodings and with a spring in your
step.

By Wednesday morning I am at work on the introduction
of the sermon. Experience has taught me that this may take
some considerable time. Charles Jefferson in one of the best
books written about preachers and preaching, *The Building
of the Church*, says that the stage will be arrived at when,
by assiduous practice, the sermon can be written, complete
and entire, in a single morning. As to that, and with over
twenty-six years of fairly assiduous practice, I can only say
that the time is far from having come for me. I have
written and rewritten the introduction over and over again.
Like Colette, I have known what it means to spend a
whole morning at my desk and have only a page of writing
to show for it. Yet on any long-range view, it is not labor
lost. It is part of the business of mastering the sermon-
making craft. And I have discovered that once satisfied
with the introduction, the remainder of the sermon can be
done more rapidly.

The introduction takes time because here especially considerations of style are paramount. A well-constructed

sentence is like a sharpened tool. If the sermon opens with sentences that are concise and precise, it will arouse interest and it may linger in the memory. There are occasions, of course, when the introduction may be said to write itself. It may lie to hand, ready for use, in the source material. I think of a sermon I preached on "The Wish to Escape." A clipping from *The New York Times* provided what came close to being a perfect introduction. It told how a bus driver, sixteen years in the employment of his firm, took the wheel of his vehicle and, instead of piloting it back and forth in the Bronx as he had done, week in week out for years, drove it right down to Florida. Announcing as the text, "O for the wings of a dove that I might fly away and be at rest," and with the escapade of the bus driver as an introduction, the sermon was well and truly launched. (The text reminds me of something that happened in a Scottish church. At the prayer meeting week by week there was a deacon who, in the course of his petitions, would exclaim, "O for the wings of a dove that I might fly away and be at rest." One evening, unable to stand the repetition any longer, a worshiper muttered, "Stick another feather in him, Lord, and let him go." It is a moot question whether there is a place for such an incident in a sermon.)

Or, the introduction may write itself because, following the choice of subject on Monday, the opening sentences have been forming themselves in the mind. Once, with for the subject "The Peril of Conformity," and for the text,

"Be not conformed to this world" (Rom. 12:2), I started off with a quotation from Voltaire: "Every man must be either the hammer or the anvil." Instinctively one went on to show how mankind, generally speaking, tends to fall into two classes, one small and one large—those who make history and those who are made by it, those who are creators of fact and those who are creatures of circumstance, those who put color into their environment and those who take their color from their environment. It was possible there and then, in the opening minutes of the sermon, to make the point of personal application, to raise the question, To which class do you belong?, and to bring in the text, Are you conforming to the world and its ways, or are you being transformed by the renewing of your mind?

What are the requirements in a good introduction? It should never be lengthy. Any tendency to become expansive or discursive, as if all the time in the world were at our command, must be resisted. We ought to come to grips at once and forthrightly with our subject. It should be as interesting as we can make it. When James Black set about the task of preparing the Warrack Lectures on preaching he conferred with lay folk, his intention being to secure their views as to what made for an effective sermon. They were unanimous in affirming that what they valued most was not dramatic power, not brilliance of thought and language, not logical argument, not passion, not eloquence, but *interest*. In their judgment the best preacher was the man who could engage and hold the mind with some truth that had a bearing on life, and could treat it in a living and gripping fashion.[5] Nowhere is this more imperative than in the introduction of the sermon. If what we say at the outset is tedious and remote, the congregation, though outwardly respectful, will soon withdraw its attention. But in aiming at arresting speech—and this is where judgment and discrimination are factors in effective preaching—we have to avoid whatever is *outré* or sensational.

I select in illustration of a brief and arresting introduction the opening paragraph of James Stewart's sermon on the Omnipotence of God in *The Gates of the New Life.* "What is the biggest fact in life to you at this moment? What is the real center of your universe? 'The biggest fact in life?' replies one man. 'Well, I reckon it is my home. That, for me, is the center of everything.' A very noble thing to be able to say! 'The main fact in life to me,' says a second, 'is, without any shadow of doubt, my work. If you take that away from me, you just take everything.' 'The central thing for me,' declares a third, 'is health and happiness. As long as I have that, I am quite content. I can't bear to be unhappy.' But what is your own answer?"[6] Notice here the economy in the use of words, the relevance to life, the range of interest certain to be aroused.

W. E. Sangster[7] tells of the last sermon preached by J. N. Figgis before the University of Cambridge. It was

[5] *Op. cit.,* p. 16.
[6] P. 11.
[7] *Op. cit.,* pp. 126-27.

the month of June, 1918. After four years of war the Allies were being steadily driven back. Miles which it had taken months to win were being lost in hours. Everywhere the atmosphere was tense. The specter of national defeat plagued many a mind. On entering the pulpit Figgis announced as his text Psalm 29:10: "The Lord sitteth upon the flood; yea, the Lord sitteth King for ever." He began the sermon at once with one question—"Does He?"

As an illustration of how not to begin Sangster cites the case of a preacher bent on expounding the 23rd Psalm. He began: "This psalm is written from the viewpoint of a sheep!" Could anything be more trite? Make a start of such a fatuous kind, and it will be next to impossible to do much either with your subject or your congregation.

Coming to *the body of the sermon* I follow the predetermined outline. This varies from sermon to sermon, though it has become my practice in the main to construct the sermon in two ways. I may work on what I think of as the evolutionary principle, drawing out the leading idea of the sermon, elaborating it, illustrating it, applying it. Or I may work on what has been called the three-decker principle, not with a ruling idea but with three propositions which are in turn articulated, elaborated and applied. For me the important thing is to watch the march and sequence of the thought in the *paragraphs* of the sermon. I give great care to paragraph construction—the size of the paragraph, the form of words with which it begins, the flow of the thought from paragraph to paragraph. If the sequence of thought is not easy, natural, logical, I know the sermon will be so much the poorer in its impact; it will be hard to follow, and, in consequence, difficult to remember.

⁓ About *the conclusion of the sermon* I would speak at greater length. Its importance can be measured by the oft-repeated counsel, for those who preach extemporaneously or from notes, to write it out in full and commit it to memory. This is, of course, because it presents the preacher with a final opportunity of securing a verdict from his hearers, and because last impressions are the most likely to be dominant ones. Conclusions, unlike introductions, are often too short. In the majority of cases, the reason has to do with the mismanagement of time. It is due to want of perspective and proportion in the structure of the sermon. How often one hears a sermon comprehensive and even brilliant in diagnosis but shallow and superficial in prescription! How often preachers devote the bulk of the sermon to exposition and allow only a few hurried sentences for the application! Few things could be more self-defeating.

The conclusion should corroborate, confirm, seal all that has gone before. Variety of approach is especially necessary here. In one case, the conclusion may summarize the principal points of the sermon. If the argument has been closely wrought and marked by precision of thought and sequence of ideas, it will be particularly helpful to spell out, one by one the truths propounded.

In another case, the conclusion may stress the need for

immediate and practical action. They still tell of a Sunday in Free St. George's Church, Edinburgh, when Whyte preached a powerful sermon and rounded it off after a long and dramatic pause—and you will soon discover in preaching how effective a pause can be—with a single sentence from the speech of Mark Antony in *Julius Caesar*: "Now let it work."

In yet another case, the conclusion may indicate how the heights to which we have pointed may be reached. It is not enough to say that something should be done; we have to go on to show specifically and in detail how it can be done. I remember preaching a sermon on "Putting Our Brains to Work in Religion," in which I bore down on the fact that scores of otherwise intelligent and well-informed persons are religiously illiterate. I ended by naming half a dozen books which, if perused, would dispose of any such charge. At the end of the service there were many requests for particulars about the books and a plea that the list should be printed in the church calendar.

Finally, in order to quicken the imagination and energize the will, the conclusion may cite an instance that illumines, at the same time that it summarizes and applies, the central contention of the sermon. Earlier I made a reference to the quixotic act of a New York bus driver, and how it prompted a sermon on "The Wish to Escape" based on the words, "O for the wings of a dove that I might fly away and be at rest." This is how the sermon was completed. "I think of Gethsemane, of the slumbering disciples and the agonizing Lord. He sweat as it were great drops of blood. Do you know why? He was casting about for a way of escape. 'O my Father, if it be possible, let this cup pass from me.' There, embodied in a sentence, you have the cry of burdened humanity—to flee from its Calvary and be at rest. But soon there came the steady, resolute words: 'Nevertheless not my will but Thine be done.' The Captain of our salvation faced the ordeal of Calvary. He was 'One who never turned his back but marched breast forward.' He is our great pattern of fortitude and endurance. He makes the coward spirit brave and nerves the feeble arm for fight. All the ages attest that by His presence in their hearts and lives, shrinking souls are made strong, and timid souls are made valiant, and they who else would take to their heels and run, are rooted and grounded in their task."

Think, then, of the making of the sermon as an art. Take the right kind of pride in your craftsmanship. At the launching of the *Queen Mary*, a riveter, his chest out and his head up, was heard to say as the great ship slipped down the stocks into the river, "I put bolts into her." Make it a fixed rule as you face Sunday morning and the pulpit to be in a position to say, "I will not offer unto the Lord my God that which doth cost me nothing."

INDEX

❦

99